God Still Does Miracles

Servants of Christ and Stewards of the
Mysteries of God

God Still Does Miracles

by
Linda Delgado

God Still Does Miracles
Copyright © 2023—Linda Delgado
ALL RIGHTS RESERVED

Unless otherwise noted, all Scripture references are from the *Holy Bible, New King James Version*, copyright © 1979, 1980, 1982, 1990 by Thomas Nelson, Inc., Nashville, Tennessee. References marked KJV are from *The Holy Bible, King James Version*, public domain. References marked NIV are from *The Holy Bible, New International Version*, copyright © 1973, 1978, 1984, 2011 by Biblica, Colorado Springs, Colorado. References marked TPT are from *The Passion Translation*®, copyright © 2017 by BroadStreet Publishing® Group, LLC, Savage, Minnesota. References marked NASB are from the *New American Standard Bible*, copyright © 1960, 1962, 1963, 1968, 1971, 1972, 1973, 1975, 1977 by the Lockman Foundation, La Habra, California. References marked NLT are from *The Holy Bible, New Living Translation*, copyright © 1996, 2004, 2007 by Tyndale House Foundation. Used by permission of Tyndale House Publishers, Inc., Carol Stream, Illinois. References marked BSB are from the *Berean Study Bible* © 2016, 2018 by Bible Hub. References marked TLB are from *The Living Bible* paraphrased by Kenneth Taylor, copyright © 1971 by Tyndale House Publishers, Inc., Wheaton, Illinois. All rights reserved. Used by permission.

Photos throughout by Linda Delgado

Published by:

McDougal & Associates
18896 Greenwell Springs Road
Greenwell Springs, LA 70739
www.ThePublishedWord.com

McDougal & Associates is dedicated to spreading the Gospel of the Lord Jesus Christ to as many people as possible in the shortest time possible.

ISBN: Trade Paper Version 978-1-950398-95-9
Case Laminate Version 978-1-960398-96-6

Printed on demand in the U.S., the U.K., Australia
For Worldwide Distrand ibution

DEDICATION

I dedicate this book to all the faithful members of All Nations Worship Center throughout all these thirty-nine years. You are the absolute best. God sent all of you to support us financially, to love us unconditionally, and to send us to the nations to minister. You will be richly rewarded by our heavenly Father. You are all part of the harvest of souls that received salvation, the baptism of the Holy Spirit, deliverance, healings, and miracles. WE LOVE YOU!

I leave this book as a legacy of my life story to my two sons, their wives, and my grandchildren. Walk in the ways of the Lord. He has chosen you for great things!

CONTENTS

FOREWORD 10
INTRODUCTION...11

1. A GODLY HERITAGE..15
2. MY SIBLINGS 20
3. MY SPIRITUAL FORMATION 25
4. LEARNING TO WORK 28
5. BORN AGAIN...30
6. CAMPMEETING AT CHAMA, NEW MEXICO 32
7. THE CALL TO MINISTRY 35
8. GALVESTON 37
9. WHAT'S NEXT?..42
10. MOTHERHOOD..44
11. MINISTRY...48
12. AND ALL WERE SAVED 53
13. STEPPING OUT 55
14. DESIRE THE BEST GIFTS......................................57
15. SO MANY MIRACLES 62
16. HEALINGS AND DELIVERANCES 84
17. VISIONS..88
18. DON'T TOUCH GOD'S ANOINTED! 94
10. DELIVERANCE FROM A FAMILIAR SPIRIT 97
20. THE SPIRIT OF DISCERNMENT..........................102
21. DREAMS ABOUT CLEANING HOUSES...............104

22. SUBMIT TO THE AUTHORITIES 108
23. IT'S NEVER EASY TO SAY GOODBYE! 111
24. APOSTLESHIP 114
25. TELEVISION MINISTRY 116
26. COSTA RICA 122
27. A CRY FOR HELP! 125
28. IGLESIA TORRE FUERTE 128
29. THE COCONUT HARVEST AND THE CURSE OF POVERTY DESTROYED! 134
30. OH, NO! THE KNIVES ARE ON THE COUNTER! .. 139
31. THE LORD TOLD ME, "SING NEW SONGS!" 142
32. COLORS REPRESENT ANOINTINGS 147
33. GRANDCHILDREN ARE THE BEST 154
34. MY POWER IS GONE 160
35. WHAT AN UNUSUAL DELIVERANCE! 162
36. DIVINE PROTECTION 163
37. BUT SHE NEEDS A DOCTOR! 168
38. A WORD OF KNOWLEDGE 170
39. NABOTH 172
40. WOW! A SPECIAL GIFT! 176
41. CAIRO, EGYPT 179
42. ON TO ISRAEL 182
43. GUATEMALA 188
44. TRANSFORMATION 181
45. OUR SILVER ANNIVERSARY 195
46. EL SALVADOR 196
47. GOD'S AWESOME TOUCH 199
48. A VICTORY DANCE 205

49. WALKING IN SANTIAGO, CHILE 209
50. PARAGUAY 214
51. TRYING TO WEAR US OUT 216
52. ON THE VERGE OF DEATH 218
53. DREAMS OF LIFE 220
54. COUNTRIES THAT I WILL GO TO IN THE
    FUTURE 226
55. A DISTINCTION OVER ME................................ 230
56. GOD GAVE ME A DESIRE OF MY HEART 234
57. HEAVENLY VISIONS... 238
58. THE HEAVENLY CHOIR 242
59. THE GREAT FEAST 245

    AUTHOR CONTACT INFORMATION 249

FOREWORD

Linda Delgado, thank you so much for always speaking positive and godly love into my life. Your covering over my life has always been seeds of blessing that are more than I can handle. I've grown so much in my faith and in my life just by the love of God that I have seen demonstrated by the two of you.

Your prayers have been a faith changer for me. Seeing God move in my life has been an inspiration and has given me a humbled heart. I am able to serve God with fear and understanding. The love of the Father God ministers to my heart daily on behalf of your prayers.

Things that you speak come to pass before my eyes. The peace and understanding of knowing that God is with me surpasses all things in this life. I've learned to bless things and people that come against me and to practice love above all because the peace of God is too valuable to lose in life.

I love you both. Thanks for being a light to my path as I'm growing with God. I pray that God continues to give you the strength, love, and hedge of protection to spread the Word of God. God bless you, Pastors!

Usvaldo Alvarez

INTRODUCTION

Many people today are away from God. Some don't even believe in Him anymore. They were raised in a Christian home but are no longer walking with God. Maybe you have never heard the Gospel of Jesus and don't know Him. He is real and the Word of God is truth. Jesus said:

> *I am the way, the truth and the life. No one comes to the Father, except through me.* John 14:6, KJV

Today others are discouraged and have no hope because they believed for an answer to a prayer request or a financial breakthrough, or for their healing, needing an answer, and it hasn't come yet. Don't give up! God has a time when He will be glorified in your life.

MIX FAITH WITH GOD'S PROMISES FOR YOU! ALL OF GOD'S PROMISES ARE YES AND AMEN!

Our lives are like a garden. Whatever we plant will grow. Words, actions, and decisions are seeds that will give us success or failure. We must get rid of the weeds (sin and mistakes) and water the seed (reading and studying the Word of God). The Word is our manual. Then, we must let the garden receive sunshine (the Holy Spirit enlightening us with revelation and direction through prayer). Then we reproduce what God has done in our lives by sharing with others, thus propagating new plants in other people's lives.

> *The LORD will guide you always;*
> *he will satisfy your needs in a sun-scorched land*
> *and will strengthen your frame.*
> *You will be like a well-watered garden,*
> *like a spring whose waters never fail.* Isaiah 58:11, NIV

INTRODUCTION

I am writing this book to share healings, miracles, deliverances, dreams, visions, and other testimonies that have happened in my own life and ministry.

Jesus Christ is the same yesterday, today, and forever. Hebrews 13:8

TO GOD BE ALL OF THE GLORY FOR CHOOSING ME TO SERVE HIM!

*"For I know the plans
I have for you," declares
the Lord, "plans to
prosper you and not to
harm you, plans to give
you hope
and a future."*

—Jeremiah 29:11, NIV

Chapter 1

A GODLY HERITAGE

I was number ten of twelve children born to my parents, Ted and Mary Barry, in the small town of Durango, Colorado. Tuesday's child is full of grace, and I have seen the grace and favor of God with me since I was a child.

My father's great-great-grandfather, James, came from Ireland in the 1800s. Dad's father, Antonio, was a schoolteacher in Sunnyside and loved to study the Bible. His mother was from Sicily, Italy.

Both of my mother's parents came from Spain and were Presbyterians. My parents and my grandfather Barry loved and served God.

Grandfather Antonio died when I was four, so I don't remember him, and I never knew any of my other grandparents. They were all deceased before I was born. Now that I have ten grandchildren of my own and love spending time with them and seeing them grow, I wish I had known my own grandparents.

My mother, Mary, was a beautiful, sweet, and kind lady who was a great inspiration to me in her daily life. Not only was she a good role model; she was also a hard worker, a good cook, seamstress, and housekeeper. She was never idle or lazy.

In the summers, my mom would do a lot of gardening. She loved to plant peas, onions, carrots, and other vegetables. And canning was a yearly chore. My sister, Josie, and I would peel fruit such as pears and peaches to enjoy fruit for the year. Then we would peel tomatoes so Mother could make her delicious salsa to can in Mason jars. In August, we would roast and peel New Mexico Hatch green chili (my hands burned for a few days afterward). Mother would divide the chili into freezer bags and put them in our freezer.

Dad would buy a bushel of fresh corn, and my sister and I took off the corn husks and washed the corn before it was frozen.

Mom was always prepared with food for our large family year-round. She would make fresh bread and home-made donuts, cinnamon rolls, fruit cake, homemade apple pies in the fall, cherry pies in July and apricot pies in August from the trees in our backyard. She grew rhubarb in her garden to make rhubarb pies. She loved to try new recipes.

I am so thankful because Mother taught me to love God and to fear Him. As I grew up, she would always have Christian music playing in our small home. She was blessed with a beautiful voice, and she often sang solos in our church. When I was a child, she would read a Bible story to me every night before I went to sleep.

People would call Mother to ask for prayer, and she would have prayer meetings in our home.

Dad worked at a company in our town that mined vanadium and later as a miner in Ouray. He worked hard to provide for our family. When he went to work in the mine, he would stay in a cabin in the beautiful mountains of Ouray. It is known as "the Switzerland of North America." He would come home on weekends and study on Saturday nights to teach Sunday School the next day. He was also the church secretary.

Dad was a hard worker, and he would do repairs that needed to be done at home. I remember him spray-painting the outside of our home. In winter, when it snowed a lot, he would climb up on the roof to knock the snow off so the roof wouldn't cave in.

He would also do repairs on his car. He used to love to go to the car dealerships to look at the new cars on his days off.

Dad had a good sense of humor and loved his family. I have always been a happy person and love to laugh. When I was quiet, he would tell me, "Come on, Linda, laugh! I'll give you a nickel."

After I received my driver's permit at the age of fifteen, he took me to the country roads to teach me how to drive. He had just bought a brand-new Ford LTD, and I asked his permission to go for a drive. He pointed to the LTD logo on the car and said, "Do you see this? It says, "Let Teddy drive!" Only after I received my driver's license was I allowed to use his car.

I never heard my parents argue. They both had mild temperaments. That was a great blessing.

Chapter 2

MY SIBLINGS

My oldest brother, Sam, left home when I was very small, and I have no memory of him. Dan, the second oldest brother, had already left Colorado and moved to California when I was born.

My oldest sister, Ruth, went to Bible school in California when I was just eleven. My sisters, Alice and Frances, went to Fort Lewis College in Durango, so I was closer to Anna, Henry, Josie, and Bobby. My brother, Tony, and sister, Debbie, are younger than I.

As a child, I enjoyed playing outside every day. I had a cat named Snowball, and I would dress her up in a little outfit that belonged to my doll, Terry. Then I would take her in my brother's red wagon for a ride up the sidewalk in front of our house. The minute her ride started, she would jump out and squirm out of her dress.

I loved to go roller skating up our sidewalk and would be having such a good time, and then our neighbor, Delia, would come out of her house and shoo me away. I would go to the park that was two blocks away and continue skating.

Another time I was riding my bicycle and a boy from across the street, Freddie Wayne, wanted me to give him a ride. He hopped on, but there was a hill behind our house, and when we went down it, we crashed. Freddie Wayne got up and ran home crying. He lived across the street from us. A few minutes later, his mom, Ida, came running to our house, and she was angry. She told Mom that her son's knees were scraped, and it was my fault.

My brother, Henry, was so much fun. One day he called Ida on the phone and asked her if her refrigerator was running. Her reply was, "Yes." Henry then told her,

"Well, you'd better go catch it!" Then, click, he'd hang up, and we would all laugh.

Another time he called Ida, faking an accent and told her, "Congratulations!"

She asked, "Why?"

He said, "You've just won some manure!"

Her next question was, "What is that?"

He told her she could use it to make her grass green. Ida had an accent, and she was quite a character.

In winter, we would go out our back door, take our sled to the little hill behind our house, and go sledding. When we were older, we would climb the big hill that was in front of our house just a block and a half away. It was a longer, winding road. I miss the four seasons that I enjoyed for eighteen years living in Colorado.

My sisters, Anna and Josie, and I would go up the hill and look down at our beautiful town. Then we would buy a Coke for a dime at the gas station. The returned empty bottles were worth a nickel for our next Coke.

One time we went for our walk up the hill, and Anna took out a pack of Marlboro cigarettes. She gave us each one and lit them. I didn't know how to puff and inhale, so I gagged and didn't want to learn how to smoke. And I never did. Anna was the one that picked my first boyfriend, the one who gave me my first kiss.

When I was seven, I started taking piano lessons on Saturdays from a red-haired teacher named Mrs. Limbri. She always had a scarf on her head and a BAND-AID® on her nose. I always wondered why she had that BAND-AID®, but I never asked.

Later, I took lessons from Mrs. Evenson. She lived by the High School on 3rd Avenue. I would walk the several blocks there every Saturday. It was such a beautiful avenue, lined with beautiful Victorian homes.

I would practice playing the piano almost every day because my older sister, Frances, could play classical music, and she was excellent. I was determined to be just as good as she. I learned to sight read the Thompson piano books, and then I learned to play by ear.

Mom would have to scrub the carpet where I got it dirty from playing the piano so much.

My siblings, friends from the neighborhood, and I were always outside playing Mother May I, 1, 2, 3 Red Light, Hide and Seek, Dodge Ball, Softball, and Badminton, and we would shoot baskets into my brothers basketball hoop in a game of Horse in our backyard.

We had a small old wooden house in our backyard that my grandfather had built, and we would play church in it. I have had several dreams about that little house, and it's always big in my dreams.

Chapter 3

MY SPIRITUAL FORMATION

From the time I was born, our family always went to Jerusalem Assembly of God Church. It was just half a block away from our home. I loved the platform of the church, for there was a full-color mural of Jesus after His resurrection. I can still picture it in my mind to this day.

I loved to go to church, but the only thing that I didn't like was that they were always changing pastors. It was good that one pastor left because one of his sons was sexually abusing girls from the church.

One time I went to church for Missionettes, his son came out exposing himself. I yelled "I'm going to tell your dad!" and ran out of the church. The fear of the Lord has long been in my life to expose darkness. Exposing sin can lead to the repentance of the individual if they're willing. If not, they will have to endure the consequences.

My Mother loved to go hear the different speakers that came to our area, and I would go with her and Dad. I attended meetings of the ministries of A.A. Allen, T.L. Osborn, and W.V. Grant and others and saw healings and miracles from a young age. I wanted God to use me to heal the sick too.

When I saw photos of T.L. and Daisy Osborn in Africa ministering to the tribes, I wanted to go to Africa and be a missionary doing the same thing. Would my day ever come?

Chapter 4

LEARNING TO WORK

When I was about ten, I started working, doing everything from baby-sitting to cleaning Mrs. Daniel's home. She would pick me up on some Saturday mornings in her big pink Cadillac. I would do easy work, and she would always give me $20.

I also cleaned an office for Mr. Mason, a lawyer, two times a week. His office was on 2nd Avenue, and I would walk several blocks to get there. One Saturday, my dad had to help me clean the big picture window on the outside of the building because it was on a slope.

I cleaned another dentist's office on Saturdays for quite a few months. I had been noticing a spot on the carpet that wouldn't come out, even though I scrubbed and scrubbed it. So, I thought that I would try to clean the spot with Clorox®. Sadly, I didn't know that it would bleach the whole area.

About two weeks later, the dentist, Dr. Anderson, moved his practice to a new location in a brand-new building. He never mentioned my big boo boo.

After I received my social security card, I worked in motels (Durango was and still is a tourist town), cleaning rooms during the summer and in a nursing home as an aide.

The summer after I graduated from high school, I had a job all by myself cleaning a small motel that had kitchenettes. I had to do all the laundry as well. I guess this is why I have dreams about cleaning people's homes, etc. (I will tell more of this story in my chapter on dreams.) With my earnings, I would buy my own clothes and personal necessities.

Chapter 5

BORN AGAIN

Even though I went to church, I had never really received personal salvation. When I heard the message about salvation preached by my pastors and others, it seemed too easy to just say, "God, forgive me." Plus, I was shy, so I never wanted to get up from where I was sitting and let all the people see me go forward.

Then, on April 12, at the age of sixteen, I received Jesus as my Savior. It was a Sunday night, and I went up to the altar, knelt, and cried and cried. The presence of God was so strong. When I got up from the altar everything was sooo bright! I had so much joy and so much love.

BORN AGAIN

That day I let God take away some things that I loved to do that were wrong in His eyes. To this day, I try to consistently let the Word of God and the Holy Spirit change me. I must guard the affections of my heart because they affect all that I am and all that I do.

> *Pay attention to the welfare of your innermost being, for from there flows the wellspring of life.*
> Proverbs 4:23, TPT

Come into my heart, Lord Jesus!

Chapter 6

CAMPMEETING AT CHAMA, NEW MEXICO

Our family had a cabin that my grandfather had built, and every 4th of July, we would all join people from other churches of the AG Central District for camp meeting in Chama, New Mexico. It was a fun time, seeing friends and meeting new people.

One year, the pastor's daughter invited me to go for a walk by the river during the night service. I went with her and learned that this was where girls would go to meet cute guys. We had just started walking when my neighbor from the cabin next door saw us and escorted us back to the service. I just knew that I was going to get in trouble with my dad, but all was well.

This same girl (the pastor's daughter) would play the piano at our church. Sometimes she would be sitting at the piano, and everyone could see "hickies" on her neck. She was wild. I never had been asked to play the piano in church, but God had my moment prepared.

AN ENCOUNTER WITH THE HOLY SPIRIT

I went to youth camp in the middle of July 1972, after the regular camp meeting in Chama. When the worship leader discovered that I was a pianist, I was asked to play in the opening service. I was very nervous about playing in front of so many people. After the worship, I went to our cabin, feeling that I had not done my best. I knelt down and asked God to help me, and suddenly I was filled with the baptism of the Holy Spirit and began to speak in other tongues, my heavenly language. This was a glorious experience. I now had boldness, confidence, and even more joy!

The next day I was telling some of the

youth about my experience and hugging them. A boy named Earnie, who was about thirteen, hugged me. After that, Earnie had a crush on me.

Chapter 7

THE CALL TO MINISTRY

In 1974, I graduated from Durango High School, and the next chapter of my life was about to begin. In seeking God about what I should do—go to college in Durango or what—I felt the call of God to study for the ministry.

I attended a Bible school, Latin American Bible Institute (LABI), now known as Christ Mission College (CMC), in Ysleta, Texas, close to El Paso. The power of God was so real in the chapel services. I was the pianist for the choir for three years and played the piano and organ during chapel and church services.

The choir would travel to sing in churches to promote and raise financial support for the Bible school. Those were great times!

The choir recorded an album in which I played the piano in several of the songs.

During my first year of Bible school, I met my husband to be, Robert Delgado. He was tall, dark, and handsome and very friendly. He had graduated from LABI before I attended and was visiting his sister who was in her second year there.

Chapter 8

GALVESTON

During my second year at LABI the choir traveled to Rosenberg, Texas, to sing at Robert's home church. After the Sunday morning service, he asked me if I and my friend, Veronica, who was staying with me at the host family's house, would like to go to Galveston with him and Rick and Nimrod who were staying at his house. Rick liked Veronica. So, all five of us went to Galveston Island.

I loved seeing the beautiful palm trees. Robert took us on a ferry ride. It was a very chilly afternoon in February. Robert and I started talking, and he asked me if he could write to me. I said, "Okay." Afterward, I wanted to buy a souvenir but had to hurry to get back to the home where we were staying because we had to be back in time for the night service. We arrived in Rosenberg just in time to get ready to go sing.

Galveston

When we arrived at church and were about to practice, I was informed that a lady from the choir happened to see all of us in Robert's car when we arrived in town. The guys were sitting in the front seat, and we ladies were in the back. Nevertheless, the choir director called Veronica into a meeting and kicked her out of the choir, just because that lady had seen us all in Robert's car.

This was so sad. My beautiful friend, Veronica, had been the female vocalist for the choir and had a beautiful voice. Now she was out. It was all very unfair.

I was so frightened that both my hands and knees were shaking as I played the piano that night. I thought that my dad was going to get a phone call and that I might also be dismissed from school.

When people ask me how Robert and I met, I tell them this story of "when I got in trouble." but then I say, "Not that kind of trouble!"

Our friends who liked each other and went with us on the ferry got married, and so did Robert and I, and we're all still married today.

Robert and I started writing letters to each other, and he soon asked me to marry him. In December of 1975, he went to meet my parents in Durango during Christmas break. We decided to get married the following year.

I had one more year of school and wanted to finish, so I prayed a lot for provision. I worked two jobs the summer before my wedding and bought my own wedding dress, paid for the flowers and for the wedding cake and reception.

Before we were married, I wanted to make sure that Robert was THE ONE God wanted for me, so I prayed. God gave me a dream. In the dream, I saw Robert dressed in a suit and holding a Bible at his side. He had a moustache. Through this, God gave me peace. At the time, Robert wasn't planning on being a pastor, but God had other plans. And Robert also later grew a moustache.

We were married on August 14, 1976 at 2:00 P.M. at the First Assembly Of God Church in Durango with family members present. My life of FAITH began that day and continues to the present.

Chapter 9

WHAT'S NEXT?

After I graduated, it was now time to see where we would go. Robert said the Lord told him to return to Rosenberg. The day before we left El Paso, I received a check in the mail from my income tax return, money to get to our next destination.

We arrived in Rosenberg, and as I saw the town, I said, "God, why did You send me to the ugliest part of the world?" It was too hot and humid, everything was flat, and there were no beautiful mountains and no lakes. The food, the culture ... everything was different. But the people were very friendly. I prayed that someone would plant some flowers. Today, this area of Texas is very beautiful! It quickly

WHAT'S NEXT?

became my home and has been now for the past forty-eight years, and I count myself to be blessed because of it.

Chapter 10

MOTHERHOOD

It was a Sunday morning, December 24, Christmas Eve, and I was getting ready to go to church when my water broke. I didn't know what was happening. A friend happened to call to check on me, and I mentioned what had happened. She told me to go to the hospital. It was time to have my baby.

At the hospital, they induced labor because the baby didn't seem to want to come. I had no contractions. Finally, at about 10 P.M., the contractions started. I grabbed Robert's hand and wouldn't let him go. I thought I was going to die, and I wanted to die. I also thought, "I don't want to have any more kids!" Those labor pains were fierce.

MOTHERHOOD

One hour before Christmas I gave birth to our son, Robert Phillip. He weighed 6 pounds, 5 ounces. He was precious, with a lot of hair that was perfectly in place. Everywhere we would go people would stop us and comment on his hair and how cute he was. We took him home in a Christmas stocking that was so big he got lost in it.

It's amazing how, after a mother sees her child, she forgets about the suffering. A year and a half later, I was in the same hospital ready to have my second child. I had a bad cough, and one of the times I coughed, my water broke. Again, I had no labor pains, and labor was induced. Still, my baby wouldn't come.

The doctor wanted to go play golf, and so I was stabbed with shots in my spine several times. When the doctor was finally pulling out our son, Robert said the baby was turning blue. Finally, David Jeremy was born. I hadn't suffered any labor pains at all, but I had back pain for years from those injections.

Eventually, God sent a pastor to preach at our church, and he gave a word of knowledge that someone was having back pain. He prayed for me, and all that pain left.

David Jeremy weighed 6 pounds, twelve ounces. He was jaundiced, so he had to stay in the hospital for a couple of days. It was a horrible feeling to leave him there. I went home crying.

Big brother Phil had stayed at his grandmother's house, and when they brought him back to our home, he turned his face and didn't want to see me. He was thinking, "You abandoned me!"

It was a lot of hard work taking care of two small children, but I loved being a mother. Robert would come home from work and see me with both boys on my lap, and he would say, "Put them down." I was always with them.

When David was born, we moved to our first home, a house that had just been built in Needville, and that was where our two sons grew up. I'm so glad they were friends and playmates.

MOTHERHOOD

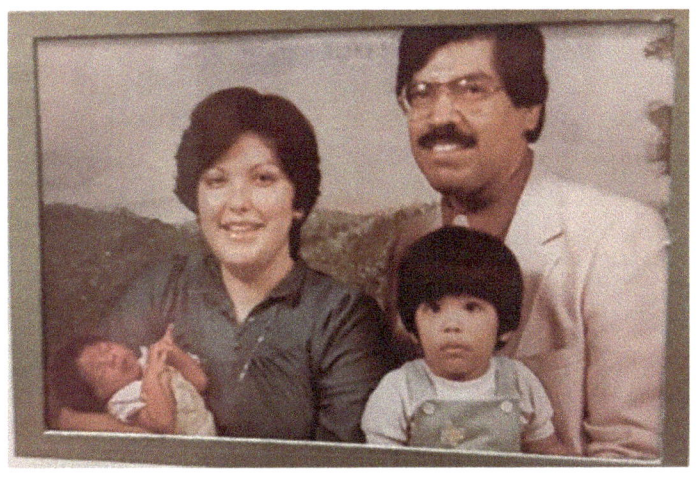

I love my sons and thank God for them. They were never rebellious and would bring all their friends to play at our house. Robert would take the boys and some of their friends to school in the mornings. He would have them get in a circle, and he prayed with them before school. One of their friends said he would have the songs that were on KSBJ, the Christian radio station, in his head all day.

Mike, one of our sons' friend, would stay at our house a lot, and he started attending our church. He brought his mom, brothers, grandma, cousins, and aunts to our church.

Chapter 11

MINISTRY

We entered full-time ministry right after we were married. A friend of Robert's, Rick Gonzalez, gave Robert a word. He had a vision of a map. God was saying that we were going to travel and not to worry about our children. They would be fine. When I would pray for them, my prayer was, "They will not go astray!"

SPIRIT OF PRAISE CHOIR

We attended Gethsemane Church in Rosenberg, where we were faithful and helping in leadership. I formed a choir and began to write songs. Robert would get ideas for dramas, and we began to travel,

MINISTRY

Spirit of Praise Choir

singing in churches and presenting the dramas throughout the area. We grew to thirty-five members in our choir, which was called Spirit Of Praise.

We bought a bus, had it painted white, and even had blue carpet installed in it. It was called "La Paloma" (the dove). We would make chicken plates, tamales etc. to sell to get funds to travel.

One of our dramas was called, "Judgement Day." We presented it in English and in Spanish, "El día del juicio." Robert received it one day as he was taking a shower. It was about people standing before the Judgement Seat of Christ from the scripture in Hebrews 9:27:

> *It is appointed for man to die once and after that comes the judgement.*

The cast of characters were God (dressed in a white gown), Satan (wearing a big black cape), two demons (in red costumes with tails and pitchforks), Jesus (with a crown on His head and a white gown), people who had died—a drunkard, a rebellious youth, a drug addict, a faithful Christian woman, a child, etc.—and two angels.

Robert played the part of the devil. In the first scene, Satan would stand before God, and God would ask him, "Where have you come from, Satan?"

Satan would pull his cape in front of him and laugh: "Ha! Ha! I've come from Rosenberg (here he would say the name of the city where we were performing the drama, and he had the perfect deep voice for the part), where my agents are doing a good job destroying lives!"

Then people who hadn't received Jesus as Savior would stand before God, and God would ask Jesus if He knew them, if their names were written in the Book of Life. Jesus would say, "No!"

Then two demons would take them to Hell. There was screaming and crying: "No, give me another chance!" "Don't take me away!"

Then the ones who had accepted Christ stood before God, and they were told, "Good job! You've been faithful in the little; you will be given much. Enter into the joy of the Lord." Then two angels would escort them to Heaven, where there was applause and celebration. Many people were saved through these dramas.

Ministry in Mexico

Next we started travelling to Mexico with the choir. I raffled off a piano Robert had bought me for our 1st Wedding Anniversary, and that gave us money to travel.

At one church in Mexico City, Robert made the altar call, and many came to receive Jesus. Among them was a little boy just crying his heart out. Robert asked him what was wrong. He said, "Estoy en pecado!" The phrase, in English, means, "I'm in sin!" He received Christ that day.

In Mexico City, we saw so many miracles. In one church, there was a paralytic named Eduardo. He had been paralyzed in a soccer accident. Robert and all of us choir members prayed for him, God healed him, and he started walking little by little. Someone called his sister, who wasn't in church, and when she arrived, she fainted when she saw her brother walking. Miracles also started happening among the other people.

Someone gave Eduardo back his bamboo cane. When Robert saw that, he said, "Give me that cane!" He and the men of the choir broke it. Our pastor had said, before we left, that we were going to see miracles on that trip, and that we were going to bring back the trophies. Robert took back the broken bamboo cane and put it in the church trophy case.

Chapter 12

AND ALL WERE SAVED

Two of the Catholic churches in our area—Guadalupe in Rosenberg and St. John Fisher in Richmond, Texas—invited us to present another drama. This one was called, "Jesus, He is the Son of God." It was based on the life of Jesus, His healings, His crucifixion, His resurrection, and His ascension to Heaven. When Robert made the altar call, everyone raised their hand to receive the Lord as their Savior. THERE WAS GREAT JOY IN HEAVEN THAT DAY!

God healed a baby that had a hernia in that service at Guadalupe Catholic Church. We later heard from the priest that the parents of the baby went to Monterrey, Mexico, and because of their baby's miracle, they had faith to pray for a woman who had leukemia, and God healed her.

> *All things are possible to those who believe.* Matthew 19:16, NIV

We were blessed to record a cassette of our choir, and our sons went throughout our neighborhood distributing some of them. Many lives were touched by the anointing of the Holy Spirit through the song and drama ministry. Countless salvations and people filled with the Holy Spirit and various miracles and healings occurred over time.

Chapter 13

STEPPING OUT

After five years of ministry in the local church, our pastor, David Cruz, whom we loved very much, told Robert that the Lord had spoken to him that the ministry God had for us was too great for the four walls of his church. He saw in the Spirit that we were to leave the church and start a non-denominational church elsewhere.

It took two more years for us to step out in faith and leave the church. I was content where I was, but the moment came when I told Robert, "Okay, I'm ready!" We resigned our positions at the church, and the following week we started a church eleven miles away in our home.

Later, our pastor gave my husband an awesome scripture showing God's approval on this ministry.

> *For the bed is shorter than that a man can stretch himself on it: and the covering narrower than that he can wrap himself in it. For the LORD shall rise up as in mount Perazim, he shall be wroth as in the valley of Gibeon, that he may do his work, his strange work; and bring to pass his act, his strange act. Now therefore be ye not mockers, lest your bands be made strong: for I have heard from the LORD God of hosts a consumption, even determined upon the whole earth.*
>
> Isaiah 28:20-22, KJV

Chapter 14

DESIRE THE BEST GIFTS

When we started our church on May 6, 1984, we named it Spirit Of Praise, the same name we had given our choir. Years later, Robert changed the name to All Nations Worship Center. Robert and I have always been a team and done things together. He appointed me to be his co-pastor.

God began to open new doors, and He also began to use us more in the gifts of the Holy Spirit. I love to teach on these gifts. They are essential to the Body of Christ so that we can share them with people everywhere. God will use us mightily to do signs and wonders, just like in the book of Acts. We are to train and make disciples to do the work of the ministry.

God Still Does Miracles

First Corinthians chapters 12 and 14 speak of the nine gifts of the Holy Spirit:

There are diversities of gifts, but the same Spirit. There are differences of ministries, but the same Lord. And there are diversities of activities, but it is the same God who works all in all. But the manifestation of the Spirit is given to each one for the profit of all: for to one is given the WORD OF WISDOM through the Spirit, to another the WORD OF KNOWLEDGE through the same Spirit, to another FAITH by the same Spirit, to another gifts of HEALINGS by the same Spirit, to another the working of MIRACLES, to another PROPHECY, to another DISCERNING OF SPIRITS, to another different kinds of TONGUES, to another the INTERPRETATION OF TONGUES. But one and the same Spirit works all these things, distributing to each one individually as He wills. 1 Corinthians 12:4-11, KJV (Emphasis Mine)

Concerning prophecy and tongues:

Pursue love, and desire spiritual gifts, but especially that you may PROPHESY. For he who speaks in a tongue does not speak to men but to God, for no one understands him; however, in the Spirit he speaks mysteries. But he who prophesies speaks EDIFICATION and EXHORTATION and COMFORT to men. He who speaks in a tongue edifies himself, but HE WHO PROPHESIES EDIFIES THE CHURCH. I wish you all spoke with tongues, but even more that you PROPHESIED; for he who PROPHESIES IS GREATER than he who speaks with tongues, UNLESS indeed HE INTERPRETS, THAT THE CHURCH MAY RECEIVE EDIFICATION. 1 Corinthians 14:1-5 (Emphasis Mine)

The first gift that God gave me was tongues. As I was praying in the Spirit, there was power and a surge as the tongues came forth. It was a message from God. My pastor's wife told me that I needed to interpret the tongues. I told her, "I can't! I don't know what I said!" I asked the Lord to give me the gift of interpreting tongues, and He did.

The gift that I flow fluently in is prophecy. Prophecy is a message the Holy Spirit gives you to speak, and you speak it out by faith. As I am praying in the Spirit, He gives me a word to speak forth for individuals and for church congregations.

The key to this gift is a daily life in relationship with the Father, through prayer, fasting, reading and studying the Bible, and praying in the Spirit. This opens us up to the power of God to begin working in our lives. It is also important to walk in forgiveness and let the nine fruit of the Spirit (see Galatians 5:22) supercede the gifts.

I'VE LEARNED THAT THE BEST GIFT IS THE GIFT THAT IS NEEDED AT THE MOMENT! For example, if someone needs healing, that is the best gift. Three or four gifts can operate at the same time.

DESIRE THE BEST GIFTS

Usually, before I operate in the gifts, God gives me a vision or a dream. As you read the testimonies in this book, recognize the gifts that were in operation to bring them to pass.

> *If there is a prophet among you,*
> *I, the Lord, make Myself known to*
> *him in a vision;*
> *I speak to him in a dream.*
> **Numbers 12:6**

Chapter 15

SO MANY MIRACLES

One night I had a dream, and the Lord told me, "I give you a mandate: Heal the sick!" I also had prophetic words given to me that I would have a ministry like Kathryn Kuhlman. A friend of ours, Mrs. York, owned a seafood restaurant, and she loved prophecy, so she would invite Robert and me frequently to her restaurant to talk and eat and would never let us pay for our meal.

Mrs. York's pastor gave me a prophetic word. It was that my left hand would turn red, and when it did, everyone that I prayed for would be delivered and healed. For quite a while I kept looking at my hand, and it wasn't turning red. I did notice that my left hand would tremble with the presence of the Holy Spirit. That was what the red hand signified. The fire and power of the Holy Spirit through me would touch and speak to people in need.

I love to pray for people and encourage them. If they have a need, I immediately pray for them. People often lie when they say, "I'll pray for you." They may mean well, but then they leave, get busy, and never do it.

Robert and I went to pray for a lady who was pregnant. The doctors had told her to abort the baby because tests showed that the child had Down syndrome. We prayed and believed, and the mother carried the baby full term. She was born healthy and now she, too, is a mother.

God Still Does Miracles

There was a girl I loved very much named Betsy. She was only three years old and couldn't walk. I picked her up, laid hands on her ankles, and prayed for her, and God did the miracle. She began to walk. She is now a beautiful, sweet young lady.

Betsy

When I was in my early twenties, God gave me the gift of praying for women who couldn't bear children. I could also sense if a woman was pregnant, and I knew what the sex of the child would be. This is called discernment. At first, after I would tell a lady she was going to have a boy, I would pray almost every day that I wouldn't be made a liar. Finally, I realized that this gift was real and gained confidence in my calling. These are some of many true testimonies for the glory of God.

God Still Does Miracles

Anita is a beautiful young lady who desired a child but hadn't been able to conceive. I prayed for her, and she had a beautiful girl, Chassidy. Chassidy is now twenty-one and is known as my beautiful doll.

This testimony brought a co-worker of Anita's to our church so I could pray for her too. She got pregnant right away.

Chassidy

SO MANY MIRACLES

Pastor Kiwia and his wife had one son, Victor, who was already a teenager. I would joke with him and tell him that Victor needed a brother. He would laugh and shake his head and say, "No!" But shortly afterward his wife, Rachel, conceived a son. He would look at me, laugh, and say, "Ah, Linda, it was because of you." I can hear his voice as I share this. I joked with him again, and yes, Rachel had another son. His response was, "Linda, it was because of you." No, it was God's blessing upon him and his sweet wife.

EVEN JOKING YOU CAN BE PROPHETIC!

PRAY FOR ME! I'M HEMORRHAGING!

About twenty years ago, my neighbor, Annette, would walk her dog, Crissy, and I would see her when I walked our dog, Lady. As I got to know Annette, she confided in me that she wanted a child, but when she was a teenager, a doctor had told her that she would never be able to have children. I asked her to let me pray for her. I laid hands on her and prayed, believing that God would do the miracle.

Some months later, Annette called me and asked me to pray for her because she was hemorrhaging and didn't want to lose her baby. She hadn't told me that she was expecting. I rebuked the bleeding and prayed for a normal full-term pregnancy.

Annette and her husband built a new home, so I didn't see her anymore for a while. Then, one day some months later, Robert and I went to eat at Olive Garden in Houston. As we got up to leave, we ran into Annette and her husband. They had a baby girl in a baby carrier. Annette turned to her husband and told him, "Linda is the reason that we had our baby!"

I replied, "God gave you your precious baby. I only had faith to believe for you."

TWINS

Carol, a local pastor's wife, mentioned to me that she would never be a grandmother. She had an only son, and his wife hadn't yet been able to have a child. I mentioned to her a few times that I would pray for Diana, her daughter-in-law, to have a child, and I did.

Eventually, Carol invited me to speak to the women's group at her church. I gave my teaching, and right afterward, I told Carol to stand up and tell the women that she was going to be a grandmother. She did as I asked her to do.

I then called Diana, the daughter-in-law, up to the front. I quoted the Word of God from Psalm 113:9 to her:

> *God makes the barren mother a joyful mother of children.* (KJV)

The Holy Spirit inspired me to have her repeat it again. I did so, believing that it was done. A couple of months later, I received a phone call from Carol. It was good news: Diana was pregnant!

On August 30, 2007, Robert and I were at the hospital because our third granddaughter, Kinsey, was being born. Diana was in the same hospital at the same time, and she gave birth to twins—a beautiful girl, Abigail, and her brother, Donovan. A few weeks later, we were

God Still Does Miracles

eating at a restaurant, and Diana was there too. She came to our table with tears in her eyes, thanking me.

GOD IS SO GOOD!

A couple of years ago, the family came to visit us, and we heard for the first time the full story about the miracle of the twins. Neither the mom nor dad could have children, but God!

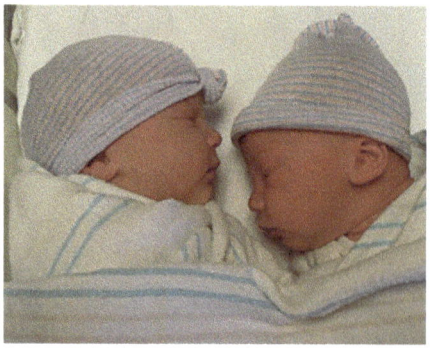

The miracle twins

The twins as teens

SO MANY MIRACLES

A MOTHER'S FAITH

Because of the testimony of the twins, a mother from Carol's church had faith to believe that God would give her daughter, Farrah, a child too. One day Robert and I were going to Cracker Barrel to eat breakfast. As we approached the entrance, Carol and a lady named Marilyn were coming out of the restaurant. Marilyn said to Carol, "It must be of God because there she is!"

Carol told us they were talking about the miracle of the twins and that they needed me to pray for Marilyn's daughter because she, too, was unable to conceive. I told the mother to have her daughter come to my house. I would gladly pray for her.

A few days later, Farrah came. I spoke Psalm 113:9 over her. A couple months later I received a phone call saying that Farrah was pregnant. She gave birth to a cute boy, Jakobe, and I've been blessed to see him every year.

God Still Does Miracles

Little Jakobe

AN IMPOTENT MAN'S TESTIMONY

One year, as we ministered in a church in Tabasco, Mexico, the Holy Spirit gave me a word of knowledge that God was going to heal impotence. I prayed a general prayer. After the service we went to eat at a couple's home. After we had eaten, the lady of the house, Carina, asked if I would pray for her to have a child. I prayed for her.

The next year, when we returned to Mexico, the couple came to our hotel with a little boy named Pablo. They shared how God had given them their son after I prayed for them. Victor, the dad, said he had been told by his doctor that he would never be able to love a woman or become a father. He had been in a diabetic coma for six months, but God did the miracle!

Victor and Carina with Pablo

DOUBLE RESTORATION

I have ministered in a lot of home services. One evening a lady, Gloria, was sharing how she had lost her son in a car crash. I prayed for her that the Holy Spirit would console her. Then the prophetic word of the Lord came to her, that God was going to give her what she had lost and a little girl.

Not long after that, she had a baby boy. She had focused on the word *girl*, and was expecting a girl. There weren't any girls in her side of the family.

The Spirit told me to go back to what I had told her. God was going to give her what she had lost. He was referring to a son.

When that baby boy was about three months old, she was pregnant again, and yes, this time it was a beautiful little girl! All glory to God!

GOD DOESN'T MAKE MISTAKES! LISTEN CAREFULLY TO THE PROPHETIC WORD!

SO MANY MIRACLES

DREAMS OF TWO SONS

One year in October a couple was travelling with us to Wisconsin. We spent the night in Missouri. That night, October 31, I had a dream, and I saw Lucia with a little boy who had curly hair. In the morning, I told her about the dream. On that trip I kept telling her to get close to her husband. They were staying in a cold place and the weather was perfect to cuddle. It snowed during that time because I had told the Lord I wanted to see some snow.

Lucia got pregnant and had a cute little boy. However, a week later he died because of an infection he had developed. That was such a difficult and sad time for them and for us. I went to the hospital, picked up the little boy (they had named him Samuel), put him in my arms and spoke life over him. I said, "Lord, you can bring him back!" but it didn't happen.

After this bad experience, Lucia had a miscarriage. The only counsel I could give her was that her two children were alive in

Heaven. When babies die, they go directly to be with their Creator.

A few years passed, and I had another dream, that Lucia was pregnant again with another boy, and she was. They named the baby Zeke. He is healthy and smart, and he plays the keyboard and saxophone.

There have been a few women I prayed for who didn't conceive. I believed for them, but I'm not God. He is the only One who knows all things. Even though we don't understand these cases, I will keep using the gifts God has given me.

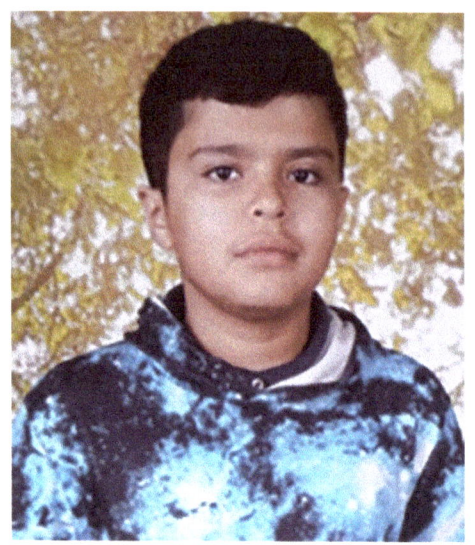

Zeke

SO MANY MIRACLES

A MIRACLE BY PHONE

A friend of mine, Pauline from Wisconsin, called me and asked if I would pray for a lady named Missi who wanted a baby. She gave me Missi's phone number. I called her and prayed for her, and she got pregnant right away. She had a beautiful little girl, Hannelore, and shortly after, a cute boy with the prettiest blonde hair. There is no distance in prayer.

I am blessed because I get to see photos of all of these beautiful gifts that God gives!

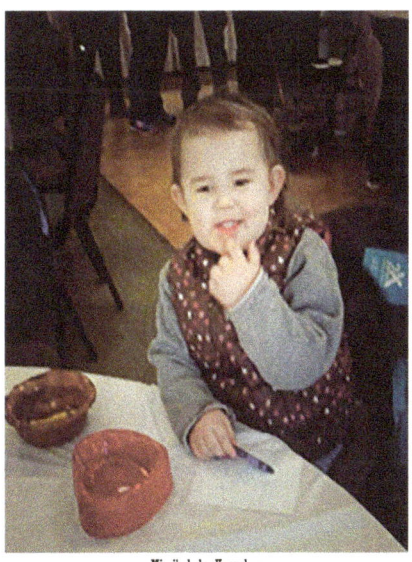

Missi's baby, Hannelore

YOUR CHILD WILL COME WHEN GOD NEEDS HIM!

A precious couple, Josue and Dory from Tampico, Mexico, couldn't have children. They were visiting us, and I felt led to pray for them to have a child. As I was praying, the prophetic word for them was that they would have a boy ... when God needed him to be born in His set time and purpose. Wow! In the Bible, Moses, John the Baptist, Jesus, and Samuel all came when it was their time to fulfill their mission.

All glory to God, David was born, and he's the cutest, smartest little boy. Every time I see his face, he radiates joy.

David

SO MANY MIRACLES

A PROPHETIC WORD OF GENDER

I prophesied to Pastor José del Carmen from Tabasco that his son's wife would have a baby girl. I then I told the son, Eloy, that God was going to give him a daughter and then a son. And God's word is faithful and true!

The pastor's beautiful youngest daughter, Carmelita, already had a daughter. I had a dream and saw that she had two boys. I texted her and told her that I didn't know if she was going to have twins or if they would be born at two different times.

She first had one little boy, Pablo Elias. That was a few years ago. Then, a few months ago, she had another boy, Samuel.

God Still Does Miracles

Bani's Son

When Pastor Garcia from Soyataco asked me to pray for his daughter, Bani, I prophesied that she would have a son. Bani had a son and named him Ronald.

Ronald

SO MANY MIRACLES

Linda's Children

Linda, a schoolteacher from Tabasco, asked me if I would pray for her. She was already close to forty and had not been able to conceive in her first marriage. She had just remarried and wanted to have a family. Shortly afterward she had a son, Jonathan, and after that, a little girl.

IT'S A BOY AND THERE'S A DOCTOR IN THE DREAM

A beautiful young lady named Peggy, someone I love so much, got married, and I had a dream about her. In the dream, I saw that she was going to have a boy, and there was a doctor standing by her side. I texted her and told her the dream. Then she and her husband came to our home, and I prayed for her just as I had seen in the dream.

As a result, Ethan was born, and doctors said he was a miracle because, at Peggy's age, his birth was a risk. During her pregnancy, she had to see a doctor because her blood pressure would get high. It's amazing how God gives us extra details!

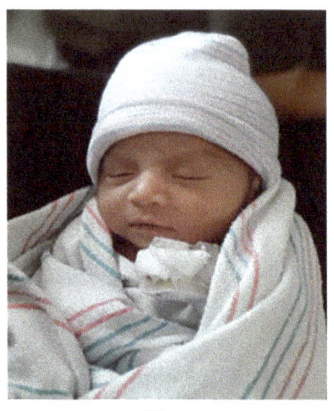

Ethan

SO MANY MIRACLES

A FACEBOOK MIRACLE

About four months ago I was going through posts on Facebook and saw a picture of a friend holding a baby. The Holy Spirit quickened me and said that she was going to have a little girl. I sent her a message and told her.

Sure enough, she found out that she was pregnant, and she had a "reveal the sex" party. Yes, my friend Marbeliz is going to have a girl. Praise God!

I had told her since last year, when she came to the U.S. from Venezuela, that God was going to bless her with an American baby girl. We sent to her baby shower this past Saturday and are excited to meet our princess. These testimonies are just a few. There are so many others. God is so good!

Chapter 16

HEALINGS AND DELIVERANCES

A MAN DELIVERED FROM ALCOHOLISM

In one of the churches in Cunduacan, Mexico I prayed for a man who was an alcoholic. It was destroying his marriage and family. A year later, when I returned to the church, he gave a testimony that God had delivered him when I prayed. He was now happy, and his family was blessed.

A MAN HEALED FROM AIDS

Last fall I received a message on Messenger. A man told me that his brother was dying and asked if I would pray for him. I called the man who had messaged me, and he put on the speaker phone so that I could pray for his brother David who was dying.

I told David that God could heal him. First, though, I led him to the Lord and had him repent of his sins. I then bound the spirit of death and prayed for his healing. I didn't hear right away if he was okay or if he had died.

Then, about three weeks ago, I received a message from a man whose name I didn't recognize. He told me I had prayed for him over the phone and that Jesus had healed him. I then remembered and knew who he was.

David said that his family had already purchased his coffin, and he was on the verge of death, but Jesus had healed Him. The second photo was taken when I called him on the phone to pray for him. He is now serving God and has a ministry in Cancún. God reveals things to him in dreams and shows him the peoples sicknesses, and he is operating in miracles.

Testimonies like these is what it's all about. Advancing the Kingdom of God ...

God Still Does Miracles

that's what I live for, to see people's lives turned around. Almost every day I pray for people and give counsel and advice.

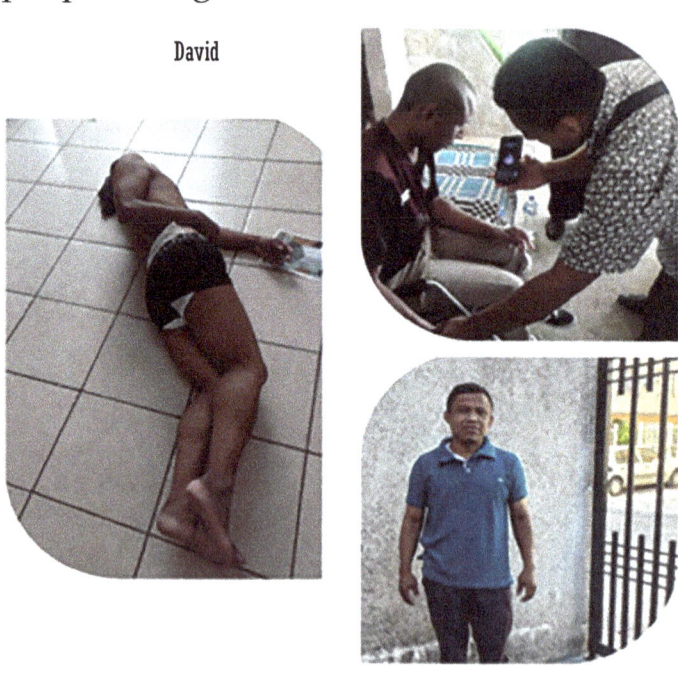

David

Healed of Kidney Problems

A lady named Eddi shared her testimony that the Lord had healed her from cancer and kidney problems. She gave me this testimony a year after I had prayed for her. There are many others, of course, that we will not know about until we get to Heaven.

Chapter 17

VISIONS

*In a dream, in a vision of the night,
when deep sleep falls on people
as they slumber in their beds,
he may speak in their ears
and terrify them with warnings.*
                    Job 33:15-16, NIV

Visions can also occur when you are awake. I've had several. When Robert and I started our church in 1984, I saw my first vision. I was at the piano, and I saw three people walk into the sanctuary—two men and a lady. The lady was in a daze. I just thought they were visitors.

When the service ended, I asked Robert if he knew the people who had been in service that day. He said there weren't any new people.

That evening he got a call to go pray for a lady who was afflicted and needed prayer. She was in a daze. I then realized that what I had seen in the morning was a vision of what was going to happen that evening. The Holy Spirit began to teach me about visions.

Another time, we had conducted a service at a lady's home and had just gotten in the car to go home when I had a vision of flashing red lights on a police car. I told Robert to slow down. A minute after I told him, the red lights of my vision became reality. Robert pulled over, and a policeman asked him if he knew he was speeding. He got a ticket that day.

OUR FIRST CALLING TO A NEW MISSION

In the late 1980s, Robert and I went to Atotonilco, Mexico to visit a newly founded work that an evangelist from our church had started. As soon as we crossed the Texas-Mexico border, I began to see visions.

I knew they were of evil spirits. I told God, "You need to show me what they are." I had continuous visions on the long trip of about eighteen hours.

When we arrived in a small town, we were happy to finally be close to our destination. Robert had stopped at the ALTO (stop sign). Then, suddenly, a dump truck that was in front of us reversed, hit the front of our gray Buick, and crumpled the hood. I yelled out, "The blood of Jesus!" and the truck stopped and sped away. The evil spirits in the land knew that we had arrived.

As we entered the village where we were going to stay and minister, it was just the way Robert had seen it in a dream of the place before the trip. (He had seen houses on the hills.)

As we drove into the site, I looked to my right, and there was a woman looking out of the window of her little casita. She was glaring at me. I waved at her, smiling. Later, we learned that she was a witch, and she didn't like the fact that we were there to evangelize and bring the Good News.

During our stay, she tried to curse us but couldn't.

Almost the entire village accepted Jesus as their Savior, and many people were healed. Our church had sent money to build a building and dig a well, and we took the children some shoes. It was an awesome work of God. The witch who tried to destroy us died because another witch cursed her.

These visions came strong because God was going to take us to Latin America, where there is a lot of witchcraft. When I minister to people, the Spirit gives me visions to direct my ministry in how to cast out devils in deliverance or for healing.

Jesus said:

And he said to them, "As you go into all the world, preach openly the wonderful news of the gospel to the entire human race! Whoever believes the good news and is baptized will be saved, and whoever does not believe the good news will be condemned. And these miracle signs will accompany those who believe: They will drive out demons in the power of my name. They will speak in tongues. They will be supernaturally protected from snakes and from drinking anything poisonous. And they will lay hands on the sick and heal them."

After saying these things, Jesus was lifted up into heaven and sat down at the place of honor at the right hand of God! And the apostles went out announcing the good news everywhere, as the Lord himself consistently worked with them, validating the message they preached with miracle-signs that accompanied them!

Mark 16:15-20, TPT

Chapter 18

DON'T TOUCH GOD'S ANOINTED!

And they overcame him by the blood of the Lamb, and by the word of their testimony.

Revelation 12:11, KJV

Yes, we overcome by the blood of the Lamb and the word of our testimony.

A young Mexican man who used to be the main drug pusher in Rosenberg asked Robert if he would teach him English. Robert agreed and had him start reading the Bible. He then accepted Jesus and grew spiritually very fast. After a couple of years, he began preaching.

About three years later, his wife left him, so he returned to Mexico where he had grown up. Sadly, he then returned to drugs.

One day this young man, fleeing from the police in Mexico came back to Texas. He came to our house drunk, and Robert went outside to talk with him. The man cursed Robert and our church. I heard him yelling outside in the yard and began interceding. He then pulled out a gun and was going to shoot it. For some reason, he couldn't, so he left.

I had a dream, and in the dream the man was in a grave trying to get out. He was also trying to pull my husband and our younger son into the grave with him.

Later, he got sick with cirrhosis of the liver. When he had started coming to church, God had healed him, but because he had returned to sin, his sickness had come back on him. Robert went and prayed for him, and the man asked for forgiveness. He died shortly afterward.

*"Do not touch My anointed ones,
And do My prophets no harm."*
Psalm 105:15

God Still Does Miracles

We are a fragrance of Christ to God among those who are being saved and among those who are perishing: to the one an aroma from death to death, to the other an aroma from life to life.
2 Corinthians 2:15-16, NASB

Chapter 19

DELIVERANCE FROM A FAMILIAR SPIRIT

For example, never sacrifice your son or daughter as a burnt offering. And do not let your people practice fortune-telling, or use sorcery, or interpret omens, or engage in witchcraft, or cast spells, or function as mediums or psychics, or call forth the spirits of the dead. Anyone who does these things is detestable to thee LORD.
     Deuteronomy 18:10-12, NLT

One Sunday afternoon, I lay down to take a nap at our home and had three visions, one after the other. The first one was of an old lady with white hair. I knew immediately that she was a witch.

The second vision was of a man dressed with a royal blue vest and matching pants. This represented the "strong man." A strong man is a principle evil spirit that has other evil spirits under him. If you cast him out, the other demons will also leave.

The third vision was of the face of an evil spirit. I asked God to show me what I was seeing, and step by step, He did.

Monday afternoon we received a call from a lady whose daughter was at school walking around in a daze. I told the mother that I wanted to pray with her. I prayed for her that evening, but she didn't get any better. I met with her two other times and was asking her questions, trying to get to the root of her condition. I eventually learned that she had gone to see a witch (the first vision I had seen).

Next, the woman mentioned that she was talking to her dead grandfather. I knew that the strong man was a familiar spirit. This was the meaning of the second vision the Holy Spirit had shown me.

On Sunday morning, I was in church when I received a call that the young lady was worse. I left church and drove to her house. She hadn't been eating, and the evil spirits in her had gained power. I commanded the familiar spirit to come out of her, and it did.

She gave a shriek and pointed at her mom, asking for access. Then the evil spirit entered her mother, and she fell on the ground rolling and screaming. When a spirit is cast out, it looks for another body to possess. I cast out the spirit and sent it to the abyss.

Afterward, the young lady was weak, and her mother wanted to take her to the hospital. I explained to her about the visions that I had seen and told her that her daughter was well and healed. She just needed to recover her strength.

She asked me what had happened to her, and I explained that the evil spirit in her daughter had entered into her body when it was cast out of the daughter.

DON'T OPEN DOORS TO THE OCCULT!

But if I cast out demons with the finger of God, surely the kingdom of God

has come upon you. When a strong man, fully armed, guards his own palace, his goods are in peace. But when a stronger than he comes upon him and overcomes him, he takes from him all his armor in which he trusted, and divides his spoils. He, who is not with Me, is against Me, and he who does not gather with Me scatters.
Luke 11:20-23

An Unclean Spirit Returns

When an unclean spirit goes out of a man, he goes through dry places, seeking rest; and finding none, he says, "I will return to my house from which I came." And when he comes, he finds it swept and put in order. Then he goes and takes with him seven other spirits more wicked than himself, and they enter and dwell there; and the last state of that man is worse than the first.
Luke 11:24-26

*IF GOD DELIVERS YOU FROM AN EVIL SPIRIT, DON'T OPEN DOORS BY SINNING AGAIN. WHY? BECAUSE SEVEN OTHER MORE WICKED SPIRITS WILL ENTER YOU!

Chapter 20

THE SPIRIT OF DISCERNMENT

A pastor and his wife came to our house with another lady. We talked and shared, and when it was time to pray, I discerned a spirit of divination. As I said that, a spirit began to manifest in the lady. She started to vomit, put her hand on her mouth and went outside and was there for quite a while.

This lady and another friend started visiting our church, and God worked in their lives. The friend who came with the lady who had the evil spirit finally came to me and shared this story.

The two ladies had been going to a local church, and their pastor was a woman. She wanted to know how to teach against witchcraft, so she went to see a witch.

THE SPIRIT OF DISCERNMENT

Because she wanted to have a large church, she was telling the people who attended her church to go visit other churches and to curse them. The Holy Spirit had exposed that foul spirit of divination.

One day Robert and I ran into that false woman who called herself a pastor. She wouldn't even look at us. God shut down her church. Thank God for the Holy Spirit who leads us and guides us and exposes the works of darkness. We are not to have anything to do with that kind of person (see 2 Timothy 3:6-9).

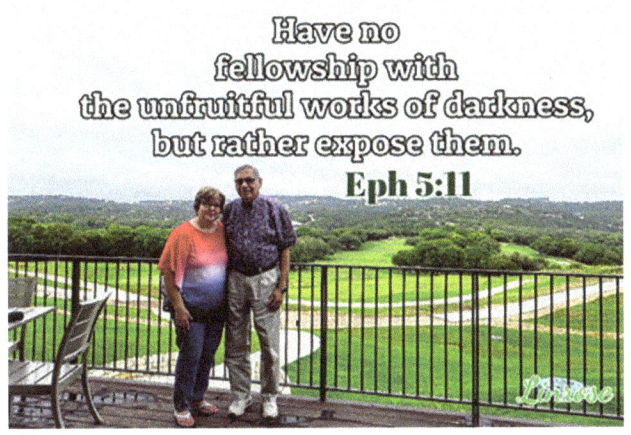

Chapter 21

DREAMS ABOUT CLEANING HOUSES

I've had several dreams over the years of going into people's homes and finding them unkept and dirty. In the dream, I start cleaning and scrubbing them. Some of the homes I have been in before and know the family that lives there, and they were very clean. But, because of the dream, I knew that I needed to intercede because there were problems in that house.

Last year, I had a dream that I went into a certain house, and it was very cluttered throughout. A couple of days later, I received a phone call to go pray at that very home. When I went into the house, it was just as I had seen it. It looked like a hoarder's home. In the natural, it needed a good cleaning and getting rid of a lot of "stuff." In the spiritual sense, only God could intervene.

I ministered to the family, giving counsel for the bad situation, and deliverance started to take place. All oppression, depression, anxiety, fear, isolation, and witchcraft were broken. The family was blessed, and things have turned around that only God could fix. They all looked so refreshed.

In another dream, I was in yet another filthy house, and I was cleaning and cleaning, even used Clorox®. There was a man in the house, and I asked him if he could help me clean, but I got no response. Then I went into another room and there was no wall. It was open to the outdoors. I could see all kinds of evil spirits outside and people possessed with them walking around. I started praying again.

People have let their guard down. They aren't seeking God, and their spiritual life no longer matters enough to them. They are letting sin into their lives. Our bodies are a temple (house) where the Spirit of God dwells. I shared this dream at a large church where I preached last year.

Another time, I had a dream of many children in a big, spacious playroom with too many toys. The children were disorganized, rebellious, and angry. Where was the parental discipline? They were using social media unsupervised.

My prayers are for our children. Wake up, parents. Your children are involved in things that you are unaware of. They don't need any more toys; they need direction, love, and your attention.

When I have these dreams, it is to send out the message of alert to parents, to the church, to bring exhortation. Jesus said, "I GIVE YOU THE KEYS OF THE KINGDOM!"

> *Whatever you bind [the work of the enemy (forbid, prohibit, declare illegal, paralyze, imprison)] will be bound in heaven and whatever you loose (allow, permit) on earth will be loosed in heaven!*
> Matthew 18:18

WE BIND EVERY SPIRIT OF SICKNESS, DISEASE, INFIRMITY, PREMATURE DEATH, AND THE SPIRIT OF FEAR AND LIES IN THE NAME OF JESUS! WE LOOSE, FAITH, MIRACLES, HEALING, TRUTH AND ABUNDANT LIFE IN THE NAME OF JESUS!

> *It is written ... With long life I will satisfy you and show you my salvation!* Psalm 91:16, KJV

Chapter 22

SUBMIT TO THE AUTHORITIES

In a dream I had recently, I was ministering to a crowd of people, and I began praying in the Spirit. The pastor approached me and said, "Don't pray in tongues!" I told him that when I pray in tongues the Holy Spirit shows me what to say, what the needs of the people are. He then let me continue to do as the Spirit was showing me, I kept on praying in tongues, and God did awesome things.

> *In the same way, the Spirit helps us in our weakness. We do not know what we ought to pray for, BUT THE SPIRIT INTERCEDES FOR US THROUGH WORDLESS GROANS.*

SUBMIT TO THE AUTHORITIES

AND HE WHO SEARCHES OUR HEARTS KNOWS THE MIND OF THE SPIRIT, BECAUSE THE SPIRIT INTERCEDES FOR GOD'S PEOPLE IN ACCORDANCE WITH THE WILL OF GOD!
Romans 8:26, NIV
(Emphasis Mine)

I've always submitted to the authority in the churches where we minister. When we were in Santiago, Chile, for example, the pastor saw that I had on culottes when I arrived at the airport. He told Robert that I could only wear them in his house. I had worn them to be comfortable on the long trip. When I go on my missions' trips, I am prepared with the necessary clothes. I had packed dresses and skirts in my suitcase.

One time I went to a church, and on the wall, they posted a message: WOMEN ARE NOT ALLOWED TO WEAR MASCARA! At that time, I didn't have any on, but if I had been wearing it, I would have washed it off. God has a purpose for the place where we will minister, and I'm not going to mess it up by being offensive to others or being offended by their beliefs.

We have visited many churches, and wherever the door is open, we go. It is like Paul said in 1 Corinthians 9:19-20:

> *Now, even though I am free from obligations to others, I joyfully make myself a servant to all to win as many converts as possible. I became Jewish to the Jewish people to win them to the Messiah.* (TPT)

Chapter 23

IT'S NEVER EASY TO SAY GOODBYE!

My Dad had a heart attack and died in 1990 when he was mowing a neighbor's yard. He was only seventy. Then, in 1993, my mom died from cancer. She had suffered for ten years. I tell God, "Why couldn't I have been born earlier so I could have enjoyed my parents longer?"

My oldest brother, Sam, left home when he was a teenager and started hanging around with the wrong crowd. Mom would pray a lot for him, and so did I as a teenager. He would sometimes call collect from a bar and ask Mom to send him money so he could buy a bus ticket to come home. Then, when he was supposed to arrive at the bus station, he never did.

Mom never saw Sam again. A family where he worked would write to her and let her know that he was fine and a hard worker. But her prayers to see him again were never answered.

A few years ago, my oldest sister, Ruth, found him, and it was prayers answered. I talked with Sam by phone and then met him in person. He looks just like Dad, and his mannerisms are a lot like Dad's. He told me why he had left home. One day he had come home rebellious and drunk and had a gun, and Dad told him to leave. That was why he never came back.

Some sixty years later, he said to himself, "What am I doing?" He left alcohol and turned his life completely around. Mom didn't get to see him, but it is a blessing to us to have finally found him.

IF YOU HAVE A LOVED ONE WHO IS LOST, DON'T LOSE HOPE!
KEEP PRAYING FOR THEM!

IT'S NEVER EASY TO SAY GOODBYE!

My sister, Anna, was very beautiful and popular and had a lot of boyfriends. In high school, she started drinking. I remember one night that she came home and was throwing up. She graduated from high school and went to college. Later she married a pilot. She then worked for a lawyer, but the alcohol led to her destruction. She became an alcoholic, and one day I received a phone call that she had committed suicide.

Chapter 24

APOSTLESHIP

People we didn't know, when they met Robert, would tell him that he was an apostle. He was a pastor, evangelist, and teacher, but an apostle? Then, one day the Holy Spirit confirmed this election for Robert.

An apostle is someone sent by God, chosen for a specific assignment. Robert had a dream and heard the voice of God telling him that God had a work for him to do.

The Great Commission is to go into all the world and preach the Gospel to everyone. This was by God's election, not Robert's. People have oten called me "Prophetess," but I had nothing to do with my election by God. I'm just "Linda."

APOSTLESHIP

Jesus never did away with the apostles or the prophets. A prophet is just a person who hears from God, then speaks what God said, and the word spoken is confirmed. It was He who gave some to be apostles, some to be prophets, some to be evangelists and some to be pastors and teachers, to prepare His people for works of service (see Ephesians 4:11-16).

Chapter 25

TELEVISION MINISTRY

In 1984, Robert had a dream in which he saw a huge satellite dish. Later, we wuld see the reality of that dream.

In 1993, Pastor Kiwia from Tanzania, Africa asked Robert to go with him to Costa Rica because he wanted to establish a headquarters for his ministry there. Robert didn't really have a desire to go. He had met Jonas Gonzalez, who lived in Costa Rica, in Houston a few years earlier. So he called Jonas and asked if he could go for a visit. Jonas said, "Yes, come."

After Robert had made the arrangements, Pastor Kiwia changed his mind about going, so Robert decided to go anyway. He wanted our youngest son, David, to go with him. At that time, I was working as a nanny. When Robert and our son came to pick me up, Scott, my boss, said to David, "I hear that your dad is going to Costa Rica. Do you want to go with him?"

David didn't respond, but Robert said, "Yes, he does!" My boss paid for David's airline ticket.

The two of them went to Costa Rica, and it was God's plan for Robert because Jonas was going to be the door that God had for him to be on television. In this way, God used Pastor Kiwia to get Robert to his destiny.

In 1995 Robert was chosen to be a coordinator for television programs for Latin America for TBN/ENLACE (meaning LINK) at Channel 14 in Houston. Robert appointed me to be co-host of the women's programs. I had learned Spanish growing up and then studied it in high school, but now I had to improve my Spanish and learn more of the commonly used phrases.

Our work for TBN/ENLACE was an amazing ten years of meeting wonderful people, hearing awesome testimonies, and ministering to a vast audience. Robert coordinated programs for children, youth, and women.

In preparation for any program, I would read and study God's Word, and when we would record the programs, everything that I had studied was the area that was touched on by our guests. The anointing flowed so wonderfully.

After ten years in Houston, Robert went to San Antonio for six years, and I also helped him with the TV program, "Fiesta Celestial," for TBN/ENLACE

Those sixteen years of television opened the doors for us to go and minister in Central and South America. Television is very expensive, but we didn't have to pay anything at all to share the Gospel in this wonderful way.

Prophet George Rojas had prophesied to us five years before it all started that we would be on television and would not have to pay anything. What a miracle! These broadcasts were a mission project of TBN for Latin America.

TELEVISION MINISTRY

For many years, the programs, "Diles" and "Dile a las Americas," were the #1 programs in Latin America. Eventually the programs were seen around the world!

Robert was a guest on TBN with Dr. Paul Crouch three different times, and I went with him to Dallas. TBN paid for the airfare and hotel and gave us a $60 meal allowance each time. They even had a limo that picked us up. God is so good!

With Paul Crouch

With T.D. and Serita Jakes

Chapter 26

COSTA RICA

Robert went several times to Costa Rica to the summit of pastors that did television ministry. I was blessed to go three times. It is a beautiful country, and we have some amazing friends that we love there who have taken us sightseeing. Raul and Adita are the best hosts.

We went on a suspended bridge and were above the trees. I saw crocodiles for the first time. The Cara monkeys are so cute, but they're thieves. We went there to celebrate our 42nd Anniversary, and Robert was invited to preach at a local church.

Kelwin was our driver, and as we were talking, he mentioned that he wanted a little girl. He and his wife had two sons. I prayed with him for a little girl, and God blessed him and his wife with a beautiful daughter, Isabella.

Isabella

Chapter 27

A CRY FOR HELP!

In 2004, a couple from Toronto, Canada (that we didn't know) saw Robert and me on television and recommended us to a ministry in Mexico. The government had asked for help from the evangelical community to stem the crisis of youth suicides. We got in touch with the director, Ramon, and went to Via Hermosa, Tabasco, Mexico for the first time to be part of "Por Amor A Tabasco." (For the Love of Tabasco.) Seventeen different ministries were being sent to the seventeen municipalities in that part of Mexico. Robert and I were sent to Jalpa de Mendez.

Pastor José del Carmen, Pastor of Iglesia Torre Fuerte (Strong Tower Church) helped us with the outdoor event held in the town plaza for a full week. His church helped us with the sound system, the praise and worship team, the musicians, and setting up the chairs etc.

On Monday evening, the first night of the crusade, at 7 p.m., the sky got dark, and it was very windy. The plaza was very busy with people. Among them, you could see lunatics and people in need of salvation and deliverance. There was spiritual warfare in the heavenlies, as this area was where witches and warlocks went to get higher powers by transforming into animals.

Then, on Thursday evening, as I was ready to minister, God brought rain to the area. The people in the plaza seemed mersmerized! I spoke on the breakdown of the family unit and how Jesus was the answer. I then prophesied over the city with the people listening. THIS BROUGHT A SHIFT, A VICTORY FOR THAT WHOLE AREA!

Different people said could see angels and demons fighting in the heavenlies that week.

A CRY FOR HELP!

The people who walked in darkness
Have seen a great light;
Those who dwelt in the land of the
shadow of death,
Upon them a light has shined.
                                    Isaiah 9:2

Jalpa de Méndez, Tabasco, México

Chapter 28

IGLESIA TORRE FUERTE

Pastor José asked Robert if he would be a spiritual covering for his church, and he accepted. We became very close to the people and are known there as prophets because of the prophetic word that was given and fulfilled.

Before Pastor José was a believer, he was an alcoholic at the point of giving up on life. He had decided to hang himself and actually put a rope around his neck. Just then, there was a knock at the door. A man needed him to fix his car. This man told José about AA. He himself had gone there for help because he, too, was an alcoholic. THIS WAS GOD'S DIVINE INTERVENTION! José went to AA for treatment and then became a leader in the organization.

Then José began having dreams that he was healing people. He started visiting different churches, but none of them had anything going on like in his dreams. He began reading the Bible, received salvation, and then started having home services. People would stop by his home, and God began using him for healing and for delivering the lost. He has an awesome ministry, and we love him and his family dearly!

Since 2004 we have been going back and forth to Mexico and have seen the lost receive salvation, tremendous healings, and mass deliverances. We have given prophetic words to that area that have come to pass, and others that will be fulfilled in God's timing.

On one visit, the pastor had just picked us up at the airport in Via, and I had a vision of some property for Torre Fuerte. The way I described it was exactly what God gave them. The pastor received the prophetic word and told the people that he wasn't going to look for the property; God was going to do it.

Then one day a man went to his house and told him that had heard they needed some property. The pastor went to see the land, and it was exactly as I had seen it in the vision. The owner of the land went down on the price, and they were able to purchase it. Hallelujah!

Torre Fuerte Church has a rehab center for alcoholics and drug addicts. On the land, they grow their own vegetables, have a pond full of tilapia, and raise turkeys and chickens. They are building a large church building, and it will be completely finished soon for the big harvest that is coming.

From the first day we arrived in Jalpa, we ministered deliverance. A dear lady had just lost her son. We went to her house, and outside, in her yard, demons manifested and came out. Why do people get demons? In that area, it's because they go to visit the *curanderos* (witches and warlocks). When the presence of God is near, the evil spirits manifest.

The first commandment is: *"You shall have no other gods before Me"* (Exodus 20:3). When people go to another source, such as a fortuneteller, physic, or astrologer, they are opening a door to the occult.

God did so many miracles among the churches in Tabasco and Campeche. We love all of the pastors there: in Amatitan, Francis and José, Pastor Amadeo and Santa in Soyataco, Pastor Josue and Petrona in Cunduacan, and all of the congregations in Campeche. They opened their doors to us and received our ministry.

Strong Tower Christian Church

Chapter 29

THE COCONUT HARVEST AND THE CURSE OF POVERTY DESTROYED!

In Paraiso, Mexico, Pastor José went to the beach to baptize new converts in water. A couple who lived on the property heard the beautiful singing and went to investigate. They heard the sermon, received the message of the Gospel, and accepted Jesus as their Savior. When the pastor left their home, he was driving, and the wheels on his car fell off. The enemy was mad and tried to destroy him.

The lady who had received Jesus and been delivered, lived on the property where her grandfather had lived before he died. He was a warlock. Many people would go to him for counsel. As a result, there was a curse of poverty on the land. It was seemingly beautiful land, but nothing would grow on it. When the granddaughter received salvation, that curse was broken. Now, the coconut trees are growing in large quantities, and the family is blessed. They eat from what the land produces, and they have fresh fish that continuously come in season from the ocean. When we go, we enjoy everything that grows there.

I prayed for Cecilia to have a baby. As I put my hands on her belly, the Holy Spirit gave her a word: people used to go to her grandfather for false help, but she was going to have a boy, and God was going to use him mightily with His gifts that are genuine. She had a son. His name is Josue. May the Lord use him mightily!

Cecilia and Joshue

Cecilia's husband, Freddy, has an awesome testimony. He had a lot of rotten teeth, and God filled them with gold, all except one. He asked the Lord why He hadn't filled that other tooth, and His answer was so that he would always remember what God had done.

In our church years ago, the presence of God was so powerful that we had people receiving gold fillings or even a bridge. One lady received a solid gold tooth. People also received gold dust. A couple of the ladies went to work and had gold dust on them. IT WAS THE GLORY OF GOD!

On another visit to Paraiso, three years ago, Cecilia said she couldn't sleep and was in severe pain with gallstones. A doctor told her that she needed to have surgery, but it was too expensive, so she couldn't afford it. I prayed for her, and she was healed.

We have so many good memories of all our trips to Mexico. We especially love the people. They are the best, very loving and hospitable.

God Still Does Miracles

Behold, how good and how pleasant it is
For brethren to dwell together in unity! Psalm 133:1

We are all members of the Body of Christ, and we must work together. In God's Kingdom, we are all different, but let's flow together and win the lost!

Chapter 30

OH, NO! THE KNIVES ARE ON THE COUNTER!

Once, when Robert was going out of town on a trip, he told me that a lady was coming to stay at our house. She was coming for an event that Pastor Kiwia had. Robert left, and the lady arrived that evening. When we had all gone to bed, I heard her walking back and forth in the halls for quite a while.

I remembered that a drawer from the kitchen cabinets had broken, and I had put it on the kitchen counter. The problem was that it had knives in it.

When I heard that she was in the kitchen area, I went and told my two sons to get up and come to my room. They did, and I continued to listen to hear where the lady was in the house. When she went into the bedroom where she was staying, I went quietly to the kitchen, picked up the drawer full of knives, and took them to my room. I locked the door and didn't get much sleep that night because I was praying. The next morning, the lady left.

When my husband came home, I told him what had happened. He said he knew she needed deliverance. I told him, "Never again! Don't bring people like that into our home!" This was before God taught me deliverance. Now I just say, "COME OUT IN THE NAME OF JESUS!"

Do not rejoice in this, that the spirits are subject to you, but rather rejoice because your names are written in heaven. Luke 10:20

Chapter 31

THE LORD TOLD ME, "SING NEW SONGS!"

When we started our church, the Lord spoke to me and told me to sing new songs. He gave me the following scriptures:

> ***Sing to the L***ORD ***a new song.***
> Psalm 96:1, 98:1, 149:1, and Isaiah 42:10

> ***Sing to Him a new song.***
> Psalm 33:3

> ***I will sing a new song to You, O God.*** Psalm 144:9

All thirty-nine of these years being pastors, we have sung new worship songs by various artists, oldies but goodies, songs in English, Spanish, and Hebrew, and songs that I have written. I choose songs that have a message.

God gave me some special ladies and men who have been with us all these years to be part of the worship team. They are faithful, anointed, and committed. We also harmonize well. Thank you, Esther, Janie, Frances, Anita, Pastor, and Brother Frank. I love you. You are the best!

New songs speak of what God wants to say now, currently, a fresh word. At times, I read a passage from the Bible and then compose a song from it. Or, if God has done something in my life, I write it down on paper. If I don't sing it, I receive new lyrics to the same melody. It seemed to me that God was saying, "Sing it already!" I have written more than seventy songs that we sing at All Nations Worship Center. I have many other song lyrics written to be developed.

There was a period last year that I would sing songs to the Lord during the night. They were just for Him. Afterward, I didn't remember them. I love to sing songs in the Spirit and also with understanding.

> *I will pray with the spirit, and I will also pray with the understanding [the interpretation the Holy Spirit puts in my mind]; I will sing with the spirit, and I will also sing with the understanding [interpretation the Holy Spirit puts in my mind].*
> 1 Corinthians 14:15

I also sing songs to my dog, just for her.

I encourage praise and worship leaders in every church I visit to pray so that they can write the songs that the Holy Spirit has for their congregation, and they will be anointed to glorify God.

> *I will also clothe her priests with salvation,*
> *And her saints shall shout aloud for joy.* Psalm 132:16

Chapter 32

COLORS REPRESENT ANOINTINGS

THE WHITE SUIT

Years ago, I dreamed that I was in Mexico prophesying to Pastor del Carmen. He had on a white suit. We went to Jalpa, and I prophesied the word of the Lord given in that dream. The message was that he would go from city to city and from state to state, moving up into the United States. Everywhere he went, the poor, the blind, and the lame would receive the Good News of salvation and the miracle they needed. It happened in that way, and his ministry grew. He eventually visited and preached in New York, then Texas, Wisconsin, and Minnesota.

God Still Does Miracles

White represents purity and light. As ministers of God, we need to live lives that please God. The Bible mentions linen, one hundred and four times. Linen is made from flax. Jesus was wrapped in linen when He was embalmed for burial. The priests in the Old Testament were clothed in linen garments (see Exodus 28). In Ezekiel 9 and 10 and Daniel 10 and 12, angels were wearing linen garments. Revelation 15 speaks of the martyrs dressed in linen.

Ezekiel 44 says that the priests will be dressed in linen garments in the future temple that will be built in Jerusalem. Let us all be cclothed with righteousness.

THE GALA DRESSES

When God is about to do something in my life and ministry, I have dreams in which He dresses me in different colors. In one dream, a couple of ladies from our church were with me at Dillards, and we were trying on beautiful dresses. We had all chosen different colors and styles. The

COLORS REPRESENT ANOINTINGS

Lord was showing us that we are royalty, and He was pleased with us. Just as He chose Queen Esther for His purpose in His Kingdom in her time, He chose us for such a time as this. We then found some shoes and jewelry.

With each color, there is a different level of authority and anointing.

> *I will rejoice greatly in the LORD; my soul will exult in my God. For He has clothed me with garments of salvation. He has wrapped me with a robe of righteousness as a bridegroom decks himself with a garland, and as a bride adorns himself with a garland, and as a bride adorns herself with her jewels.* Isaiah 61:10, BSB

Always remember that we are all in different stages in our walk with God. Some are seeking Him more. Some spend more time in the Word and in prayer, so they receive more revelation. When were open for more, the Spirit gives to us as He desires.

SHE'S WEARING MY RED DRESS!

In one dream, I was wearing a red dress. Another worship leader I know put on the same dress, and it fit her perfectly. This was

COLORS REPRESENT ANOINTINGS

interesting because she wears a dress two sizes smaller than I do, but somehow this red dress fit her perfectly.

The meaning of that dream was a transfer of my anointing to her. She now carries the same anointing that I have. She has the same passion and love for worship as I do. Glory to God!

Never be lazy in your work, but serve the Lord enthusiastically.
Romans 12:11, TLB

Be aglow! Let others see Jesus in all that you do! Shine for Him! Give Him your best, and all the glory belongs to Him!

THE GOLD DRESS

I've always had favor, and certain women from our church have blessed me with dresses, shoes, jewelry, and money. In a dream, Sister Rachel (our #1 giver) gave me a gold dress. It was symbolic of having gone through testing and trials and bearing wounds.

God Still Does Miracles

Rachel

I had gone through a period of sadness, slander, lies, and accusations spoken against me. Such wounds hurt, and only God can mend a broken heart and bring healing. I had to forgive and forgive and forgive some more.

But God always blesses me. He's been my Best Friend, my Confidant, my Strength, my Defender, and my Protector. He is the strength of my life, my Savior, my Healer, my Everything!

Robert and I belong to a ministerial alliance (CMC), they chose different pastors

COLORS REPRESENT ANOINTINGS

and leaders in ministry to be honored as GENERALS OF GOD, and we were chosen. It was a big event that took place at Grace Community Church in Houston. They honored us for doing Christian television for sixteen years, our ministry of missions and evangelism to the nations, fifty-six years of full-time ministry for Robert and forty-seven for me. They showed a video of our ministry and gave us a plaque and trophy and a monetary gift. We so were grateful!

Chapter 33

GRANDCHILDREN ARE THE BEST

I had asked the Lord to give me two sons and two daughters when I got married. He gave me the two sons, but then my husband didn't want to have more children, so I began to pray that God would give me granddaughters.

Both of our sons married beautiful young ladies. My daughter-in-law, Jen, had heard me saying that I wanted granddaughters, and she told my husband, "Tell Mom that we don't want a girl; we want a boy!"

Right away, I said, "I'm not going to be a meddling mother-in-law." I never had thought about what *they* wanted. I told my son, David, "Okay, David, you can give me the granddaughters." Well, Jen had three daughters—Sydney, Riley, and Kinsey.

I had a dream that Phil and Jen were going to have a boy. Then they received Mo, a little foster boy who was two years old, and Jen became pregnant with our grandson, Jeremiah. In time, they adopted Mo, and later they went to China and adopted another boy named Luke.

I told my younger son, David, that God was going to give him a boy. David married Desiree, who already had a daughter, Makena, and a son, Kalen. When Desiree got pregnant, I thought it was going to be the boy I had told David he was going to have. I was wrong. It was a girl (Saige), and the next year they had another girl (Everleigh). God knows all things, and when I told David that God was going to give him a son, I was right because He gave him Kalen.

When I told him he could have girls, he did. The only problem was that I didn't ask Desiree what *she* wanted. 🙂

God Still Does Miracles

I love my sons, my beautiful daughters-in-law, and all of my ten grandchildren. They are beautiful, talented, and smart kids.

Our oldest son, Phil, is a pastor and a firefighter. Our youngest son, David, works with computers and is a buyer/planner. I'm so thankful for God's divine protection for both our sons.

David went to work in Iraq during the war. One night as I was sleeping, I had a vision in a dream. I saw a bomb exploding.

GRANDCHILDREN ARE THE BEST

I woke up and thought of my son and began to intercede for him. The next morning, I received a call from someone who had talked to him on the phone. He told them about the bombing and said that he was safe. God is so good because He protects our children and also our grandchildren.

> *The angel of the L*ORD *encamps around those who fear him,*
> *And delivers them.* Psalm 34:7

God Still Does Miracles

My granddaughters and I have had a lot of tea parties, good memories for all of us. This past year my two daughters-in-law joined us.

And, meet my sweet fur baby. She's hyper, smart, and super-fast!

Chapter 34

MY POWER IS GONE

A man brought his son to our home so that Robert could pray for him. Robert talked with him and gave him counsel. He then anointed him with oil. The young man left and went home, banging his head on the wall. He was angry because his powers were gone. He had been involved in yoga and the occult.

His dad called and wanted to bring him for more prayer. I felt to anoint our house with oil and declare that no evil spirit would enter our home. The young man came back with his dad, but he went to the rest room and stayed in there a long time. I went to my bedroom and was led to pray in the Spirit.

When the young man came out, he left. I felt in my spirit that had he wanted to do harm but couldn't. There are people who want to stay in their sin and don't think that certain things they have gotten involved in will bring evil spirits. They need to be informed about what God detests. Yoga invokes a false god. With each move and chant, a person is invoking the evil spirit. I share this because some Christians do yoga as exercise and don't know how dangerous it is.

Chapter 35

WHAT AN UNUSUAL DELIVERANCE!

One night, at a meeting in Wisconsin, I prayed for a man and placed my hands in the specific area that the Spirit led me to. I had one hand on his lower back and one on his stomach. Suddenly, the strangest thing happened. His back became hollow, and it was as if he had a hole in his back. The evil spirit was pushing his stomach forward, and it was bloating in and out like a pregnant woman. It was so strange and kept moving like that until the spirit or spirits came out. As a child this man had killed cats and done some other bizarre things, BUT JESUS CAME TO SET THE CAPTIVES FREE!

Chapter 36

DIVINE PROTECTION

About seven years ago, Robert and I went to visit the missions close to Ciudad Victoria, Mexico. We drove our car to the border and then took a bus to our destination. Once we had crossed the border, we started hearing stories of how the cartel was kidnapping people, robbing them, and then killing them. They even found buses buried with people still in them.

When we were nearing San Fernando where the cartel was active, God sent a downpour of rain. I told Martha, our church missionary, "Do you see what God just did for us?" We had heard that when a bus would arrive in San Fernando, the cartel would go inside and rob or kill the people.

God Still Does Miracles

Because of the downpour, no one came into our bus.

We arrived at the bus stop in Ciudad Victoria, and the Pastors Carrillo were there to pick us up. We went to their *ranchito* in the boondocks (in the middle of nowhere). Their house had no electricity, and yet they were obeying God's call to evangelize that area.

One morning the pastor took us to see seven different *ranchitos* that they had evangelized. We had just gone a few miles, and I noticed a beautiful hacienda with a white picket fence. I asked the pastor who owned that home. He said that a leader of the cartel owned it, but he had just been murdered.

Suddenly, my eyes saw an army truck full of soldiers with guns pointed at us. Were they soldiers or the cartel? At the time, the cartel members were dressing like soldiers, so it was sometimes hard to tell. A man dressed in uniform came up to the car and told us to get out.

My mind was asking, "Is it my time to become a martyr?" We got out of the car,

DIVINE PROTECTION

and he asked us what we were doing there. We told him that we were visiting the area. Thank God they let us go!

Right behind the first truck, there was another truck full of soldiers. God had put them there to protect us!

At one of the *ranchitos*, I prayed for a lady who couldn't have a baby. The next year I received the news that she had a child.

The seventh *ranchito* was a colony of witches. We shared the Gospel there. After we ministered the Word, Robert prayed for a girl who was deaf and dumb. Little by little, she began to hear and also to speak. Hallelujah! She learned to say Jesus in Spanish and in English!

The nights we stayed at the pastor's home, the dogs would be barking and growling, and we did a lot of praying. Robert had a dream that evil people were outside trying to get into the property, but they couldn't because God had blinded them.

When we arrived back at Reynosa, we stayed at Pastor Yanez's home. We were outside on his terrace, praying and singing, and I had a long, live vision. It was animated, and in it I saw witches doing a dance against Robert and myself. I saw a big, healthy plant dry up. They were cursing us, BUT THEY COULDN'T CURSE WHAT GOD HAD BLESSED! The enemy tried to put fear in me, but I overcame it.

DIVINE PROTECTION

When we returned home, we heard on the news that a lady from Texas had been in that area with her husband doing mission work, and the mafia had killed her. I was very grateful to be home and safe. THERE'S NO PLACE LIKE HOME!

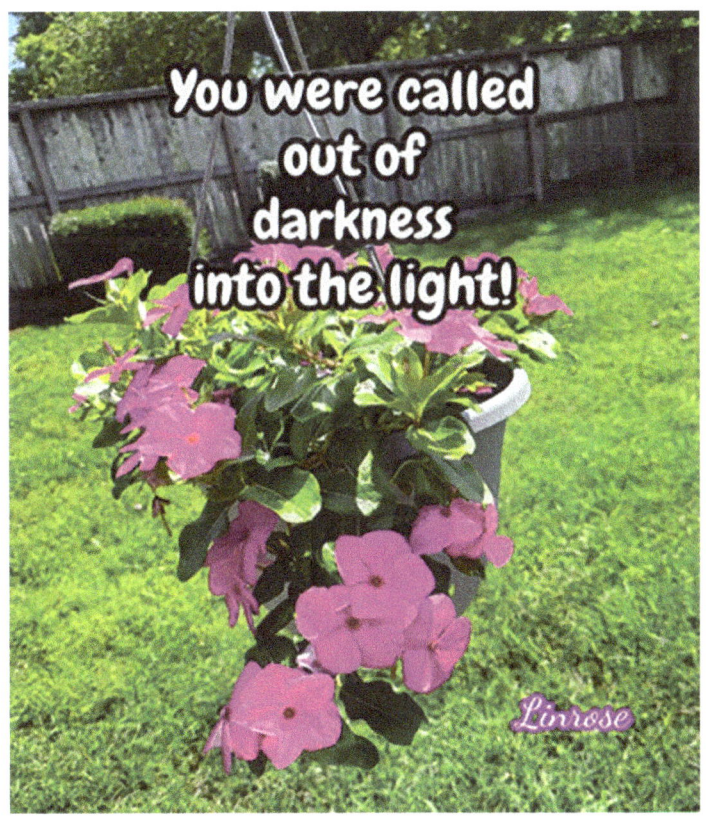

Chapter 37

BUT SHE NEEDS A DOCTOR!

At one of our yearly conferences in Tabasco, I was enjoying the worship when a deaconess called me to go pray for a lady who was having trouble breathing. I prayed and prayed, and nothing was happening. One of the church members, a lady, was a doctor. I thought, "The doctor needs to pray for her. What if she's having a heart attack."

I asked the deaconess if she would call the doctor. She told me the doctor was in the church office doing a live radio program. So, I continued praying. A powerful spirit in this woman was coming out, but in the process it was choking her.

I did not give up, and it finally came out. She was slain in the Spirit and set free.

BUT SHE NEEDS A DOCTOR!

In ministering deliverance, you must be persistent. DON'T QUIT UNTIL THE VICTORY COMES!

Chapter 38

A WORD OF KNOWLEDGE

Several years ago, when we were visiting some special friends in Wisconsin, I went to get my hair cut at our friend, Sue's, shop. Stacy, a midget, had a special platform to stand on, and she did my hair. It was interesting because I had never met a little person before.

We talked, and I asked her about her father. She told me that she hadn't heard from him in a long time. I ministered to her and just let the Spirit lead me in everything I said.

Before I left, I prayed for her and told her that her dad was going to call her. Later, I heard from my friend that her dad called her that same evening. She was telling others that I was a psychic. I'm not! That was the gifts of the Holy Spirit in operation. I told my friend, who was a Christian, to tell her about the gifts that God gives.

Chapter 39

NABOTH

Robert and I were invited to go minister at a conference in Phoenix, Arizona. As I was seeking the Lord about what I should teach, I had a dream, and the Lord gave me one word—NABOTH. I knew who the man was, so now I refreshed my memory by reading the story in the Bible. It is found in 1 Kings 21.

Naboth, the Jezreelite, owned a vineyard, and King Ahab coveted his vineyard and tried to buy it, but was not successful. The king was at home, and Jezebel, his wife, told him, "Why are you so angry and upset about not getting that vineyard? You're the king. If you want it, I'll get it for you."

She wrote letters and put the king's seal on them. She had lies spread about Naboth,

NABOTH

saying that he had cursed God and the king. Angered, the people stoned Naboth to death. Then, however, the prophet Elijah came with a word from the Lord:

> *Then the word of the LORD came to Elijah the Tishbite: "Go down to meet Ahab king of Israel, who rules in Samaria. He is now in Naboth's vineyard, where he has gone to take possession of it. Say to him, 'This is what the LORD says: Have you not murdered a man and seized his property?' Then say to him, 'This is what the LORD says: In the place where dogs licked up Naboth's blood, dogs will lick up your blood—yes, yours!'"* 1 Kings 21:17, NIV

The moment to share my teaching arrived, and I shared the message the Holy Spirit had given me about the "Spirit of Jezebel" and how it was out to steal ministries. I spoke the things that God wanted me to share. After the morning meeting, the pastor, a well-known prophet in the area, called me into his office. He asked me where I had received the impartation I had. I told him that the Holy Spirit was my Teacher. He said that I had all nine gifts operating in my ministry. He shared with me that two people had tried to steal his ministry and bring division to the church. The word of the Lord was confirmed.

He asked Robert to minister in the evening service. Robert preached and raised an offering for the pastor of the church (as he always does when we travel). The pastor testified that he owed a large amount of money to the IRS, and the offering was enough to pay off that debt.

When we were invited to be speakers, we were promised an offering of $1,500. We have never gone to minister for offerings nor charged a certain amount of money for our ministry. If we are given an offering, praise God. The person in charge of the finances said that not enough money had come in, so we would not be receiving an offering. We didn't get upset about that because God has always been our Provider.

Another couple that ministered on TBN were also invited guests. They were very upset, so they were given their $1,500. We didn't want to get involved in the gossip, so we stayed out of it.

The night that Robert ministered, the church didn't give him an offering, and it was a church of about a thousand members. The "spirit of Jezebel" was what was going on in that church, and God had exposed it.

Chapter 40

WOW! A SPECIAL GIFT!

In November of 1995, Robert took the TV programs from Channel 14 in Houston to San Salvador, El Salvador, for ENLACE. On Sunday night, the day before he left, he was led to tell our congregation that just as God was taking him to El Salvador for the first time, God was also going to take him to Israel.

He was in the green room of Channel 25 (where the guests meet before being on the TV programs), and there he met a couple. He shared with them about a prophetic dream he had. The next day he received a phone call from the lady, Loti. She asked if she could meet with him on Thursday. He agreed.

WOW! A SPECIAL GIFT!

Two days passed, and Robert met Loti. She said that she and her husband were impressed with the dream, and they wanted to give him a trip to Israel. They were the owners of a travel agency. The amazing part was that they were giving me a free trip too.

The two-week trip was called The Second Exodus. It was to start in Cairo, Egypt and take the route of the Israelites leaving Egypt and going back to the Promised Land.

The first week of February 1996, Robert and I boarded a flight to Miami to get our connecting flight. We met Loti at the Miami airport, and she also gave us $300 spending money. Isn't God amazing! The word that Robert had given at church was fulfilled four days later, and then we were blessed at the airport.

We had an all-night flight, so I decided to take off my shoes. In the morning, when we arrived in Paris, France, I tried to put my shoes back on, and they didn't fit. My feet were swollen. I had to carry my shoes and walk without them through the airport.

We were to have a six-hour layover there, so we decided to walk outside and see a little of the city. It was snowing, and we didn't have coats. They were packed in our suitcases.

I was finally able to put on my shoes, and we started walking and then got on a superfast subway. We tried conversing with a few people, but they were rude and didn't want to give us any information.

When we arrived across from Notre Dame, it was a beautiful sight. Even though it was snowing, we saw some beautiful tulips and other flowers outside.

I was surprised to see graffiti on some of the buildings. I managed to find a refrigerator magnet to take home. It was of a hill with flowers that said PARIS. Unfortunately, years later, it fell off of the fridge and broke.

We hurried back to the airport so we wouldn't miss our flight to Cairo. Arriving at the airport, we saw the famous Concord, the fastest passenger jet ever. As we flew enroute to Cairo, we flew over the beautiful, snow-capped Alps.

Chapter 41

CAIRO, EGYPT

We arrived in Cairo at about 8 P.M. and stayed in the beautiful Cairo Marriott, originally the exclusive Gezirah Palace Hotel. We had to quickly freshen up and get ready for a welcome dinner for all the people who were part of our tour group. Interestingly, Robert and I were the only Americans. The others were from Central and South America. Everyone was very tired from the long trip, but we enjoyed getting to know each other.

The next day we were up early and off to see the Nile River. We saw a reenactment from Exodus of the story of baby Moses in a the basket hidden in the tall grass. It was very windy that day, and the dust storms were strong. Robert and I had to buy scarves to cover our faces. He said the people all looked like they had sleep in their eyes.

Next, we went to the Great Pyramids. As we got off of the tour bus, I saw camels for the first time. What unique animals!

There were children everywhere selling souvenirs. They spoke in different languages. They would do their best to put a chain around your neck or bracelets and rings on your hands, hoping to make a sale.

The most famous of the Egyptian pyramids are those found at Giza, on the outskirts of Cairo. Several of the Giza pyramids are counted among the largest structures ever built. The Great Pyramid of Khufu is the largest Egyptian pyramid. It is the only one of the Seven Wonders of the Ancient World still in existence, and is the oldest wonder by about two thousand years. It had a small opening, and people could go inside, but not me. The entrance was too small and claustrophobic.

The guide said the pyramids had preservative factors and could keep grain for long periods of time. Even milk would not spoil in

CAIRO, EGYPT

there. Some, he said, go there to seek higher powers. The only power I sensed there was a spirit of oppression and darkness.

The Great Sphinx of Giza is a limestone statue of a reclining sphinx, a mythical creature with the head of a human and the body of a lion. Facing directly from west to east, it stands on the Giza Plateau on the west bank of the Nile River. The face of the Sphinx appears to represent the Pharaoh Khafre.

I never thought that I would go to Egypt, but God is awesome. It was a wonderful experience!

Chapter 42

ON TO ISRAEL

Getting ready to leave Egypt, we boarded a tour bus to continue our trip of the exodus of God's people to Israel, the Promised Land, the Holy Land. On the way, we passed through the Suez Canal. It is an artificial sea-level waterway connecting the Mediterranean Sea to the Red Sea through the Isthmus of Suez and dividing Africa and Asia.

Our travel guide did a great job letting us know of the Bible events that took place in the areas we were traversing. For instance, we passed through Marah where the water had been bitter, Moses threw in a tree, and the springs were made sweet.

We saw Elim, which means "large trees" — a place of seventy palm trees growing by twelve springs of water. Our tour guide asked us if there were still just seventy palm trees. These palms and springs represented the fullness of God's blessing for His people after a long, hard journey. The story is found in Exodus 15:27.

We spent the night at Mt. Sinai. Some of the tour group climbed the mountain, but Robert and I didn't risk it because it was too dark.

We stopped at the Dead Sea where you can float on top of the water because of the salt content. We were told that a person can only stay in the water for twenty minutes at a time. Many products are made from the minerals of the Dead Sea, such as lotions and cosmetics, and are now on sale there and around the world.

Some of the people who were in the tour group chose to be baptized in the Jordan River. They had been baptized in water before but wanted to do it again. They also took water from the river in little bottles as a souvenir. Robert and I didn't take any.

When we arrived in Israel, there was such

an awesome feeling of peace, beauty, and joy. The water was so blue. THE BIBLE CAME ALIVE AS WE VISITED THE SITES WHERE JESUS' MINISTRY HAD TAKEN PLACE!

We had to wash our clothes, and the hotel charged us $100. We were so glad we had the cash given to us in Miami.

We visited Capernaum, the city in the Galilee where Jesus had lived. He healed a paralytic there, and the story is found in the synoptic gospels.

We went to Bethlehem where Jesus was born. There were various shrines that have been erected there over the centuries. Bethlehem is also known as the City of David.

In Jerusalem, we visited the Mount of Olives, named for olive groves that once dotted its slopes. From there, we could see a panoramic view of the Holy City. Jesus taught His disciples on this mount. Matthew 24 and 25, about the end-times, are known as The Olivet Discourse. Jesus also ascended to Heaven from this mountain after His resurrection.

ON TO ISRAEL

We visited the Garden of Gethsemane where Jesus prayed the night of His betrayal and arrest. His sweat became drops of blood. Still, that night He healed the man Simon Peter had cut the ear off of with his sword.

We visited Mt. Calvary where Jesus was crucified for me and for the whole world. He took my sins and died for me so that I could have eternal life.

Robert preached at the Roman Amphitheater in Caesarea and on a boat on the Sea of Galilee. There at the Sea of Galilee (actually a lake), we ate at Peter's Fish, and everyone ordered chicken!

The lake was such a beautiful blue color. We stayed in a hotel right across the street from the water's edge.

Back in Jerusalem, we visited the Upper Room, a very nice experience because everyone was praying and worshipping.

We planted a tree there in Jerusalem. It was amazing to see the irrigation system the Israelis have developed.

And the desert shall rejoice, and blossom as the rose.
                             Isaiah 35:1, KJV

ON TO ISRAEL

We had a lot of fun and made a lot of friends on the tour bus. We always sat in the back, and Stuart and Kelwin, who were just about twelve and thirteen, always sat near us. Their parents, Raul and Adita from Costa Rica, would sit beside us. We later went to visit these friends at their home in Punta Arenas, and they were always excellent hosts, taking us to see the sights of their country, as I mentioned earlier.

Friendships were made with Sonia and her mother from El Salvador. We also later visited her in her home. It was an amazing home with balconies and a waterfall flowing in her living room. She had maids who wore uniforms and served us.

Our friends from Asuncion, Paraguay were Carlos, Rosa, and her husband, and the *"Coronel."* We went to visit them too on a trip to South America. God's family is big and wonderful.

Chapter 43

GUATEMALA

One of our good friends, Brad, has been a great blessing in our lives. He wanted to go on a missions trip with us. In the end, he paid for our trip and went with us to Guatemala.

Guatemala is such a beautiful country. Our first stop was in Guatemala City. Robert ministered there at Iglesia Principe de Paz with Pastor Muñoz. It is a large church that has five services on Sunday. He spoke in the first service at 7 A.M. and was then asked to minister at the second service at 10 A.M. God did some awesome things.

Charito, the pastor's wife, volunteered to take us sightseeing to Antigua, Guatemala's colonial capital. It is a unique town with colorful houses and cobblestone streets. The mountains and volcanoes surrounding the area were majestic. Behind the houses were beautiful gardens and restaurants where we enjoyed eating delicious Guatemalan food.

We visited a park where we walked. There was a magician performing there. He wouldn't look at me. People with evil spirits recognize the Jesus in me. He told the other three people of our party that they were Christians, but not me. Then he told me that the United States was going to fall. I began rebuking the evil spirits in him as we left.

Our next stop was Xela (pronounced sheh-la) which is four hours away from the capital. There we stayed with Pastor Juan Durini and his wife in their home.

It was very cold in Xela, and I wanted to to take a shower, but I was dreading turning on the water. I just knew it was going to be freezing cold. I was thinking, "It would be nice if someone could invent an instant heating element that could attach to the shower valve." I turned on the water, and it was the perfect temperature. Wow! I was impressed! We didn't even have that in the U.S. at the time!

Robert ministered at Juan Durini's church, and the people were blessed.

A painting of Antigua, colonial capital of Guatemala

Chapter 44

TRANSFORMATION

The next stop in Guatemala was Almolonga, Quetzaltenango. We had seen a transformation video on this town and were so happy to be able to see the miracle with our own eyes. Before the transformation, the town was full of alcoholics, and the land was cursed because of idolatry and witchcraft, and nothing would grow. There were no jobs, and very few people were educated.

There is a mountain as you enter into the town where people would make sacrifices to their idol, Maximòn. He was a three-foot idol consisting of a clay mask and a wood and cloth body. He received the kisses of the faithful who would kneel before him, placing at his feet bottles of liquor purchased with meagre earnings. The worshippers hoped against hope that their offering would bring blessing and healing. The priest offered lit cigars to the idol, and would take a mouthful of the liquor offering, spewing it over the devotees.

One day a man named Mariano Riscajche, a twenty-six year old, was so drunk that he passed out and lay drunk on the ground. When he came to, he looked up into the sky and saw Jesus. He was saying, "I love you, and I want you to serve Me." From that encounter, Mariano began reading and studying the Bible and praying. He started a church called El Calvario.

At one point he was threatened by six men. After breaking out his front teeth, they forced the barrel of a gun down his throat. They pulled the trigger of the gun three times, but when nothing happened, they were filled with fear and ran away.

In 1974, God brought transformation to the area after twenty years of prayer. The people began fasting three to four times a week and deliverance, salvation, and miracles began to occur.

The town's bars closed, crime decreased, and jails were no longer needed. It is said that ninety-seven percent of the people became born-again Christians.

The Mayans of this town today are a hard-working bunch and drive Mercedes Benz trucks full of giant vegetables. The carrots were as big as my arm. The land was healed and now produces harvests three times a year. From there, goods go out to all of Guatemala and also to other countries. It is said that the veggies grown in that place have an extra ingredient in them.

This revival has been so well documented that people from all over the world travel to Almolonga to see the amazing transformation. We were blessed to be among them.

Robert preached at Mariano's church, and he is now a friend of ours. The Mayans were dressed in beautiful outfits with beautiful embroidery. The women sat on one side of the church and the men on the other.

The church built a school up on top of the mountain for the Mayan children. We wanted to go see it, so we had to walk halfway up the mountain.

Our church donated a brand-new keyboard to the church in Almolonga because they didn't have one.

Mariano's wife, Michaela, is a tiny lady. When we met her, she had raised thirty-eight people from the dead. What an impressive trip that was!

Brad later invited Pastor Mariano to go speak in Minnesota, and Robert translated for him there. I was blessed to go along.

Chapter 45

OUR SILVER ANNIVERSARY

On August 14, 2004, Robert and I celebrated our 25th Wedding Anniversary at Lake Atitlan in Guatemala. It lies in a crater created by the great eruption of a volcano. We took a boat ride on the lake and enjoyed the beautiful view. We stayed in a hotel there. Three beautiful volcanoes surround the lake. The scenery was so beautiful, and the weather was so nice and cool, it reminded me of growing up in Colorado.

Chapter 46

EL SALVADOR

El Salvador is one of Robert's favorite countries. On one trip there, I went to Iglesia del Camino in Ciudad Merliot. After the awesome praise and worship, the pastor stood behind the pulpit and gave a testimony of three prophetic words that Robert had given to the church the year before. He had prophesied: 1). That the pastor would minister to a multitude of people, 2). That the church would be on radio, and 3). That God was going to open television to them.

Pastor Mauricio Navas said that all three of the prophecies had been fulfilled. He had ministered at the National Stadium where more than 100,000 people had attended.

They now had two radio stations operating from their church, and the third fulfillment was that they were given a television station. GLORY TO GOD!

Later, when Pastor Navas asked me to share, I got up from my seat, and the presence of God was so strong that it led me to a lady in the congregation. I put my hand on her neck and told her, "The Lord is healing you."

A couple of days later, the pastor told me, "Tomorrow night you're going to hear about the power of God in your hands."

The next night, at the church service, the lady I had laid hands on gave a testimony. She said the Lord had healed her completely from a neck injury she had suffered in a car accident. She hadn't been able to turn her neck and lived in continuous pain. She brought a copy of her X-rays before and after the healing.

HALLELUJAH! TO GOD BE ALL OF THE GLORY! JESUS IS THE HEALER!

Yes, He just wants us to follow His direction and do whatever the Spirit tells us to do. Someone you know needs a miracle. Act in faith, and use the gifts of the Holy Spirit to set them free!

Iglesia El Camino, Ciudad Merliot, El Salvador

Chapter 47

GOD'S AWESOME TOUCH

In April of 2014, we were preparing to go to El Salvador to minister. It was a Wednesday, and I started feeling terrible pain in my right breast. It continued to intensify, and when I examined my breast, I could feel a large lump there. I was getting worried, but I was in prayer.

I didn't want to tell my husband so he wouldn't worry. We were to take a flight early the next morning. I decided that if the pain didn't leave, I would stay behind and check myself into a hospital.

We had prayer at our home that night, and I asked for prayer. I still had pain. I told God, "You know that we have this trip planned, and I won't go to El

God Still Does Miracles

Salvador just to be sick or be in a hospital. Touch my body and heal me!"

I slept about an hour, and when I woke up at 1:00 A.M., I didn't feel any more pain. I still had a bit of fear, but I thanked God that the pain was gone.

We took our first flight and were at the airport in Miami waiting for our connecting flight, when I looked at my phone and saw a message from Jen Carl, a member of our church. It read, "Pastor Linda, I had a dream about you last night. You were asking prayer for yourself because you were in pain. I turned to the right and saw a man dressed in black lighting a candle, doing voodoo against you." I knew then that the enemy had been trying to keep me from going to El Salvador.

We arrived safely and I was feeling okay. That night, our driver, Victor, picked us up and drove us to the top of the mountain and we went to get some cappuccino before the evening service. When I got out of the car, I felt dizzy, unbalanced, and very tired.

We went on to the service, and it was wonderful. At that time, the country was having problems with gangs, and the people were living in fear. Some were being kidnapped and receiving threats against family members if they didn't pay large amounts of money to the gangs. We were there to pray and encourage the people. The Lord had given me a word for San Salvador, and it was televised throughout the region. THE RESULT WAS A BREAKTHROUGH!

The rest of our stay, I was very tired, but I didn't have any pain, and our mission was fulfilled.

We arrived home on May 4. The next day, I went to see my primary care doctor for my annual checkup. She did an EKG and told me that it showed something irregular. I was referred to a cardiologist. She also sent me to schedule a mammogram.

When I went to set an appointment, there was an opening to get it done at that very moment. I had it done, and in two days, I received a call that everything was normal. There was no growth in my breast! HALLELUJAH!

The day arrived to go see the cardiologist. He told me that the EKG showed that I had suffered a mild heart attack and suggestd that I go have a nuclear stress test done. I made the appointment.

Some friends of ours invited us to go with them to a service in Houston where an evangelist was going to be speaking. I really didn't want to go, but I went anyway. After the evangelist preached, he had a word of knowledge and said that the Lord had shown him that someone there had heart problems. Robert looked at me and said, "It's you!" I went to the altar. The evangelist said he had seen by the Spirit that I had a problem with my heart valve. He laid hands on me, and I was slain in the Spirit.

When I fell backward, I felt pain in my tailbone. Ouch! I had been slain before and had never felt any pain. The pastor mentioned that a witch was in the service. Now the tiredness I had been feeling for an entire month was completely gone! I HAD RECEIVED MY HEALING!

The next day was Sunday and even though I had pain in my tailbone, I went to church, played the piano, and gave the testimony of my heart attack and my healing. I hadn't told anyone about the heart attack except Robert and our two sons.

The day arrived for the stress test. When I was on the treadmill, and they injected me with meds and kicked up the speed, I had just said, "Lord, help me," and the test was already over. The technicians took pictures before and after, and in a few days, I went back to the cardiologist for the report.

HE TOLD ME THAT I WAS YOUNG INSIDE! THERE WAS NO DAMAGE, AND EVERYTHING WAS GOOD! MY HEALING WAS CONFIRMED!

After three weeks, my tailbone was healed. The enemy was mad at me getting my healing and tried to get me down, but I overcame by the blood of the Lamb and the word of my testimony!

Chapter 48

A VICTORY DANCE

Robert was invited by Pastor Alejandro Rivera to go minister in Honduras. He set the dates, and we waited in prayer for the finances for the trip to come in.

When the date to travel was a week away, we still had no funds available. We went to church on Sunday night, and during the altar call, we received a call from the police department saying that someone had broken into our apartment. When I heard that news, I did a little dance and declared, "The thief stole from us, and he has to pay us seven times more. Thank You, Jesus, for the victory!"

Right after I did that dance, a lady named Desiree went into the church office and said that she wanted to give us an offering for our trip to Honduras. It was $2,000. On Monday, Robert had our travel agent book our flight. Carolyn Rodriquez Chapa went with us, and we had a fun time.

When we were about to land in Teguzigalpa, it was on the shortest landing strip. There was a mountain, and WHOA, we barely missed hitting it. I've heard since that it is the worst airport to land at.

The services in Siguatepeque were very nice and the people were very friendly. The Holy Spirit ministered and brought edification to the people.

I ministered to a group of ladies in a conference room at the hotel where we stayed. After praise and worship, the pastors wife introduced me to the ladies so that I could bring my teaching. When I began, I raised my hand to pray, and I saw a lady fall back. She hit the concrete floor with a loud thud.w I prayed over her and gave her the word that the Holy Spirit had for her.

After that, it was hard to get my mind fixed on my message. I was wondering in the natural if she was okay. She was. It was the power of God.

I finished giving the word and prayed for the ladies, and as I was going out the door, the lady who had fallen missed a step going out of the conference room and twisted her ankle. Now she was really in pain. That night I prayed for her every time I turned in bed. The next morning, as I went walking outside, I saw the lady, talked with her, and she was fine. Praise God!

The anointing hit that lady, and she wasn't hurt, and the Spirit ministered to her life. When she fell on the step, the enemy was trying to steal her blessing, but she still had victory.

I noticed that in some businesses and restaurants where we ate, Christian music was being played and also TBN/ENLACE was on the televisions.

The church had its own TV studio, and Robert and I were guests for a program.

We went to La Ceiba on the coast and to San Pedro Sula. It was very hot, but they were beautiful places to visit. There was also a beautiful waterfall. We love Honduras.

God Still Does Miracles

Trust in the LORD, and do good:
Dwell in the land, and feed on His faithfulness.
Delight yourself also in the LORD,
And He will give you the desires of your heart.
Commit your way to the LORD,
Trust also in Him,
And He will bring it to pass.
He will bring forth your righteousness as the light,
And your justice as the noonday.
Rest in the LORD and wait patiently for Him!   Psalm 37:3-7

Chapter 49

WALKING IN SANTIAGO, CHILE

In 2000, I had a dream. I saw a big tree with gold foliage. I started walking, and I knew that I was in Santiago, Chile. I thought it was just a very interesting dream until three years later.

We had a special guest visit our church on a Sunday. Her name was Alberta. She stood behind the pulpit and said, "Pastor Delgado, I want to go with you to South America." We hadn't been to South America yet.

During lunch our guest and Robert discussed a possible trip to Chile. Robert knew the general manager for TBN/ENLACE in Santiago. He told Alberta that he would call that pastor and see if he would receive us and schedule some services where we could minister.

Our friend, Judy from Wisconsin, who had brought Alberta to minister in our church, pulled out her checkbook immediately and wrote out a check for a thousand dollars for Alberta's airfare.

Robert communicated with Pastor Edito Espinosa in Santiago, and he welcomed us and prepared an agenda for us. I kept saying, "Okay, Lord, I had the dream of walking in the streets of Santiago, and I *am* going. I need money for my plane ticket. " The trip was set for October.

When we were a week away from our departure date, neither Robert nor I had our airline tickets yet. Alberta called Robert and said that she was very sick and congested and wouldn't be able to make the trip. Judy told Robert that he could have the thousand dollars that she had given for Alberta's ticket. Praise God for that, but I was the one who had the dream. I kept saying, "I *am* going!"

Cynthia, a lady from Stafford, Texas, used to house Alberta when she was in the Houston area. She sent me a check in the mail to help pay for my ticket. Yes, I was going!

WALKING IN SANTIAGO, CHILE

When the day came to leave for Chile, we were at the George Bush International Airport in Houston at the ticket counter, the agent looked at our tickets and then asked Robert, "Did anyone ever tell you that you look like Colin Powell?"

Robert said, "Yes, a few people have told me that before."

She then asked if we would like to fly first class. We accepted and flew first class to Lima, Peru. Robert ate everything the stewardess brought. We had a layover of several hours there in Lima, and then we continued our journey.

When we arrived in Santiago, it was spring, and Chile was chilly. I was freezing! We stayed at Pastor Edito's home. He had four servants who took care of everything. I got close to Conchita, the cook. I tried to help her in the kitchen, but she would tell me, "No! You're a pastor. I need to serve you!"

The next day, I started washing dishes. Conchita didn't want me to, but I told her, *"El que no trabaja, no come!"* (He who doesn't work can't eat). I continued to help the rest of the time we were there.

We had some beautiful services in Santiago. Robert ministered and gave several words of knowledge. By the Holy Spirit, he knew that there was a lady in that church who had a son in prison. The Lord said that he was going to get out of prison miraculously and was going to serve in that church. A few months later, Robert called the pastor and asked about the man who was given that word. He said that the word was confirmed. It happened just the way Robert had said it would. Praise God!

The church had an orchestra of several children who played violins. Their music was very beautiful!

Conchita had told me that she had a husband who was diabetic and was in a wheelchair. I told her that we would love to go visit him. One afternoon we walked to her house. We shared with him, prayed for him, and gave them a love offering.

On the walk back to the pastor's home, Conchita was teary-eyed, as she thanked us for visiting her husband. She said that no one had gone to pray for him, and God had sent someone from so far to minister to him.

The pastor took us sightseeing. It was a very enjoyable time.

My dream of the gold tree was that I was going to visit Santiago when it was Autumn in Texas. The trip was worth gold because Chile is very beautiful. It has beautiful scenery, and beautiful vegetation. Even the vegetables are big. The Holy Spirit had used us to minister His purposes to many people.

We also went to Viña del Mar, an amazing city on the coast of Chile. The ocean had the most beautiful, foamy waves.

> *And the gospel must first be preached to all the nations.*
> Mark 13:10, KJV

> *And this gospel of the kingdom will be preached in the whole world as a testimony to all nations, and then the end will come.*
> Matthew 24:14, KJV

Chapter 50

PARAGUAY

After we left Chile, we flew to Paraguay to see our friends we had met on the trip to Israel. Paraguay is a poor country with cobblestone streets and a lot of red dirt. Robert ministered at a large Assembly of God church in Asunción, the capital. When he made the altar call, many young people received salvation and about thirty of them received the baptism of the Holy Spirit.

A friend of ours drove us eight hours through the desert to Filadelfia, and Robert ministered there at a Mennonite community. It was a very quaint place.

We visited with Carlos, who was a banker, and we became good friends. He later came and lived with us for six months so that he could study English.

Rosa and her husband invited us to stay at their beautiful new home they had just built. When I went to use the restroom, I had to call Robert because I didn't know how to flush the commode. He figured it out. There was a water tank mounted to the wall above the toilet, and on the side there was a little rope to pull. I had never seen one of those before.

We had a home service with Ana and her husband and stayed in their home. When we left, she blessed me with two lovely necklaces.

Chapter 51

TRYING TO WEAR US OUT

In 2014, I had a heart attack, and we got hit in the back of our red car—twice. One day Robert was close to our house, and a lady hit him from behind. She said that she blacked out, accidentally accelerated, and hit our car.

Another day, we went to a medical center to pray for a lady. On the way back, the traffic slowed down, and a lady hit us from behind. We both suffered whiplash.

A couple of years later, we were in Cancún, and a man hit from behind the car we were traveling in. A man who didn't know us told us that the devil hated us and had been trying to destroy us. He described one of the accidents. He continued to say that the enemy had tried and tried to get us out of our town, and since he hadn't been successful, now he was trying to wear us out.

Then Robert nearly died twice, but we won't leave this earth until God chooses to take us home!

Chapter 52

ON THE VERGE OF DEATH

On September 26, 2014, after a morning walk with Robert, I had to fight for his life. He began to have chest pain and pain in his arm. He called 911, and the ambulance came and took him to Methodist Hospital in Sugar Land. He had suffered a heart attack. He was in a lot of pain and felt like he was dying.

The doctors immediately put a stent in his main artery—the widow maker. It was, they said, 100% blocked. His life was spared with no damage to the heart.

A week later, he was diagnosed with prostate cancer, and shortly after he was told that the cancer was aggressive and had spread to his bones. Eleven tumors grew on his bones. He was in and out of the hospital, and was very weak and very tired and at the point of wanting to die.

The side effects from the medications and radiation were horrific. It was like a bad nightmare! Every single day, I would lay hands on him and pray for him and speak healing scriptures over him. He would then fall asleep and wake up stronger.

It has been a nine-year battle. Praise God that some of the tumors disappeared, the others are no longer active, so he has zero active tumors today!

Chapter 53

DREAMS OF LIFE

I'd like to share several dreams I had during this battle for Robert's life. In the first dream, Robert and I were walking on a ledge, and suddenly a lion jumped up and stood right in front of me. He looked straight at me. Our eyes locked and were fixed on each other. Amazingly, there was no fear, just perfect peace. The lion then jumped down, and Robert and I continued to walk.

Then two lions jumped up in front of us, one in front of me and one in front of my husband. I locked eyes with the lion in front of me, and once again I experienced total peace. The scripture came to me from Proverbs 28:1 *"THE RIGHTEOUS ARE AS BOLD AS A LION"* (KJV, Emphasis Mine).

A couple of days later, in another dream, I looked to the left, and there was a beautiful lion with a beautiful mane sitting on the second floor of the balcony of a building. He turned and looked down at me and said, "Hi there, beautiful Linda!" I had assurance and peace that God was with us.

God Still Does Miracles

Robert was so sick that he really wanted to die. One time he told me, "I've seen God do so many miracles and healings in my ministry for many people, and now it seems like I don't have faith to believe for myself."

I told him that he was feeling sick, and if he didn't have faith, I did, and I WAS GOING TO FIGHT FOR HIM!

I had yet another dream. Robert was driving his white Cadillac up a winding

hill. It was snowing, and the road was icy. I told him, "Slow down. You're a Texan, and you don't know how to drive in this kind of weather!"

When we got to the top of the hill, I knew where we were. My grandfather and my parents were buried there. Green Mount Cemetery was all covered with snow. None of the existing graves or monuments were visible.

There were a lot of people in groups talking. I started talking with someone, and when I looked for Robert, he was nowhere to be seen. I started walking to try to find him. When I finally found him, he was sitting at the end of a large folding table by himself. In front of him was a small birthday cake with one candle lit. I woke up and looked at the clock. It was 1:11 A.M.

I was awake a good while thinking about that dream. Then, first thing in the morning I was quickened by the Holy Spirit to look up Isaiah 55:10-11:

As the rain and the snow
come down from heaven,

*and do not return to it
without watering the earth
and making it bud and flourish,
so that it yields seed for the sower
and bread for the eater,
so is my word that goes out from my mouth:
It will not return to me empty,
but will accomplish what I desire
and achieve the purpose for which I sent it.* (NIV)

Then Jeremiah 1:11-12 came to me. It reads:

*Moreover the word of the LORD came to me, saying, "Jeremiah, what do you see?"
And I said, "I see a branch of an almond tree."
Then the LORD said to me, "You have seen well, for I am ready to perform My word."*

I knew then that Robert was not going to die, but live. When he woke up, I told him my dream. He said, "That means I only have one year to live because the cake only had one candle." I assured him that it would not be that way. It has now been more than four years, and he is doing well.

You will never know how hard it is to live with someone who has cancer until it happens to you. It affects every aspect of your life—your emotions, your finances, and your agenda. I had to draw strength from the Lord every single day. Pray for those you know who are suffering. Visit them and be a blessing with encouraging words and love.

Chapter 54

COUNTRIES THAT I WILL GO TO IN THE FUTURE

I have had other realistic dreams of visiting other countries. I had two dreams of going to London. In the first one, I went to visit my sister and ministered to a group of women. In the second dream, I was at a lady's house. She told me to get dressed, and I put on a very elegant dress. We then went to a gala where everyone was dressed elegantly.

I was seated at a table chatting with a lady, enjoying myself and happy, laughing like I always do. Everyone looked so beautiful in the room. After a while I looked up and saw evil in a lady's eyes.

She made a comment to the group standing with her: "Those Christians who are always laughing and SO HAPPY!" She was mocking me, and as she got nearer, I saw that her eyes were red like fire, and she was coming toward me. Suddenly, I pointed at her, with no fear, and rebuked the evil spirits and began speaking the Word of God. Immediately, she started dissolving just like in an animated movie. The other women with evil spirits also came at me, and one by one, they also dissolved.

Then, I saw a handsome man coming toward me. He had sparkling, alluring eyes that were drawing me, but I started speaking scripture over him, rebuking him. He was the head satanist. Then I woke up.

In one of my dreams about two years ago, I went out the door of my house and started walking. I walked and walked for a long time. Then a couple stopped and picked me up. I sat in the back seat of their car, and I asked them where we were going. I looked up and in front of me was a huge mountain covered with snow. The lady told me, "Milano!"

When I woke up, I told Robert about my dream. I asked him where Milano, Texas was. I remembered that on our way to Colorado we would pass through Milano. He told me, "Girl, you weren't in Milano, Texas; you were in front of the Swiss Alps in Milano, Italy! "I have told the Lord that I've gone to the countries that He has taken us to and that now I ask Him to give me a dream trip to Austria, Italy, and Switzerland. I know that we will do the work of the Kingdom there. That's just our life!

In a prayer room in Cuerna Vaca, Mexico, I had a vision and saw the word COLOMBIA written in gold letters. In God's time, I will go to Colombia.

A dream that I think about occasionally is that my husband and I and another couple were boarding a bus. We were leaving our country. I hope that never happens, but God is still in control.

More than forty years ago I had a dream that a private plane landed in Norway. Robert and I got out of the plane, and a tall farmer and his daughter met us in a field.

The harvest is ready, and God will send us to evangelize there in His timing. This dream is always in my heart.

Chapter 55

A DISTINCTION OVER ME

On October 8, 2019, when covid-19 began, I had an awesome dream. I was in a beautiful theater, like the National Theatre in San José, Costa Rica. We had just visited it two months earlier in August for our Anniversary, so it was fresh on my mind. It is a beautiful building with beautiful wood paneling and balconies with box seats.

In the dream, I walked out on the stage and started singing a song, "God is making a distinction over me." As I began singing, I looked at the faces of those present in Latin America—children, youth, and adults. Everyone in the theatre sang with me in perfect English.

When I woke up, I wrote a song with the words I had been singing in the dream.

In November, a group of us went on a missions trip to Tabasco, Mexico. I had prepared myself to bring a sermon and it was going to be a great message, but in the hotel the Holy Spirit took me in a different direction and gave a whole different message.

He had me bring a message on "The Ten Plagues Found in Exodus." I shared the scripture from Exodus 9 where the people in Goshen were protected from the plagues of flies and of hail. God made a distinction over His people.

> *And in that day I will set apart the land of Goshen, in which My people dwell, that no swarms of flies shall be there, in order that you may know that I am the L*ORD *in the midst of the land.* Exodus 8:22

God Still Does Miracles

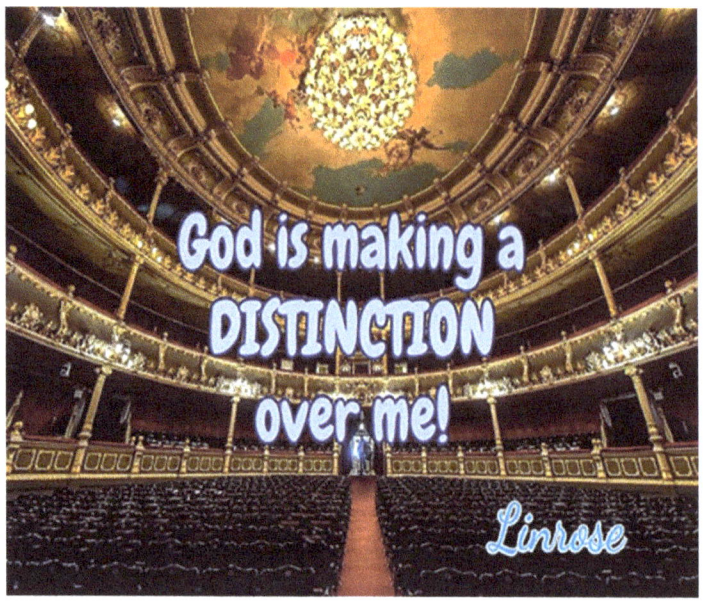

During covid we sang the song I wrote.

One night after I had this dream, I woke up, sat up in bed, and heard voices of angry men outside my window talking about me. I didn't feel good and decided to check my blood pressure. It was high. Then I couldn't breathe very well. I got up and went to the living room and began praying, rebuking every attack of the enemy, and speaking the Word of God over myself.

Eventually I called for my husband to get up and pray for me. He prayed and went back to bed, but my battle lasted for four hours. Then, I was healed. God is so good! The enemy, the devil, wanted to kill me, but God delivered me!

During covid, I lost three of my siblings. My older sister, Josie, had been diagnosed with MS in her early thirties. When covid hit, she died.

Right after Josie died, my second oldest brother, Dan, passed away, and my older brother, Bob, also died. He had a rare type of cancer in his back. The year before I had seen all of them on a trip we took to Colorado Springs. Because of the restrictions from covid, we now couldn't travel to Colorado.

Chapter 56

GOD GAVE ME A DESIRE OF MY HEART

Last year I had the desire to get away from the Texas heat and drought, and Vancouver was in my heart. Robert and I wanted to go there for our 46th Wedding Anniversary, but he was sick and going through cancer treatment.

In October of 2022, a beautiful couple that we love, Frances and Rudy, blessed us with a trip to Vancouver. They have been a huge blessing all of these years in our ministry, and we rejoice in how God has blessed them. We love you and may the Lord bless you more and more!

It was a relaxing time sightseeing. We stayed at the Hyatt Regency Hotel downtown and were close to the beach. We were

The Cuellars

able to walk and enjoy the beautiful cool weather.

Robert and I celebrated my birthday with dinner on the cruise boat, The Constitution. It was a cold night of music, great food, and meeting new people.

We went on a ferry ride and went to Butchart Gardens in Victoria, the capital of the province. As you can see, I love gardening, and many of my posts in this book are from my own garden. I chose the cover for my book from these beautiful gardens.

A friend and sister in the Lord, Mitsi Burton, called me and told me that after church that day, she had taken a nap, and the Lord gave her a dream about me.

In the dream, she saw a beautiful garden with a lot of butterflies and hummingbirds flying around in it. The Lord told her that I was not just a single flower in a garden; I was a whole beautiful garden in His Kingdom!

She then saw a clear stream with crystal water flowing. The Lord told her that my garden would be waiting for me in Heaven when I get there some day. I love gardening, and my desire is to always bear fruit in my life that will give Glory to God. Father, thank You for this awesome word. I LOVE YOU!

If I think that these pictures of the flowers from my garden were beautiful this spring and summer here on earth, I can't even begin to imagine the beauty of the flowers in Heaven

Chapter 57

HEAVENLY VISIONS

On February 24, 2023, I was at a winter camp meeting in Virginia. During the 8:00 A.M. morning prayer, I had my eyes closed and began to see visions. I saw luscious green grass, trees, and a mountain ascending to Heaven. My visions are moving, zooming in and out, very real, and cinematic.

During the 11 o'clock A.M. service, the visions continued. All day, and even during the night service, the visions were non-stop.

Green is the color of life, and I thought of Psalm 23:

The LORD is my shepherd;
I shall not want.
He makes me to lie down in GREEN PASTURES;
He leads me beside the still waters.
He restores my soul;
He leads me in the paths of righteousness
For His name's sake.
Yea, though I walk through the valley of the shadow of death,
I will fear no evil;
For You are with me;
Your rod and Your staff, they comfort me.
You prepare a table before me in the presence of my enemies;
You anoint my head with oil;
My cup runs over.
Surely goodness and mercy shall follow me
All the days of my life;
And I will dwell in the house of the LORD forever. (Emphasis Mine)

The next day, Thursday, the 25th, the visions came again. During prayer, I began to see white stones, buildings, and a wall. I was in Israel. I saw arches, portals, a stream of water in the middle and a mountain ascending into Heaven. It lasted for an hour. At the end of the vision, I saw a side profile of Jesus wearing a crown.

In the 11 o'clock A.M. service, the minute I closed my eyes the visions started again. I saw a panoramic view of a beautiful emerald color. It spanned a large area as if on a large screen. Then the color was a beautiful blue that I hadn't seen before. Then purple came into the vision. Then it was a combination of the three colors.

Emerald green is a color that symbolizes refinement, royalty, and wealth. Purple, as a color in the Bible, represents wealth or royalty. Purple dye was made from the blood of tiny sea snails from the Mediterranean Sea. Wearing purple symbolized royalty, grandeur, independence, wisdom, devotion, extravagance, pride, and creativity, just to mention a few.

HEAVENLY VISIONS

Blue represents the heavenly realm (see Exodus 24:10) and the healing power of God. It is the color of the sky, the oceans, and water.

The next vision I had that day was of white clouds of different sizes on a baby blue background. They were moving. Clouds bring shade and refreshment to our thirsty souls. They are protection from the heat.

Chapter 58

THE HEAVENLY CHOIR

Robert and I went to Detroit in 2019 to attend the Crusade Against Cancer with our friend, Apostle David E. Taylor. His ministry has always been a blessing in our lives. Everything is done with excellency, and we are treated as kings and royalty! The presence and anointing of God were so heavy in those meetings. It was the *kavod,* the heavy weight of God's glory. I love worship, and my spirit was electrified.

THE HEAVENLY CHOIR

On our flight coming home, I was exhausted and closed my eyes to try to sleep. Immediately I began to hear music and singing. It continued for about fifteen minutes. I opened my eyes and told Robert, "I'm hearing the heavenly choir." I shut my eyes again, and the singing continued.

The songs were mainly about blessing, and honor, and glory, and power in all ranges and pitches over and over in different ways. I begin to sing along with the choir. Then I would sing, and the choir would sing with me. We were in such beautiful unity and harmony, and there were such majestic voice ranges. It was an hour and a half of ecstasy. WORSHIP USHERS ONE INTO THE THRONE ROOM OF GOD!

I took this next photo while sitting in the airplane after I heard the heavenly choir. Just yesterday, as I worshipped God, His anointing came on me, and He gave me a new song, "KAVOD!"

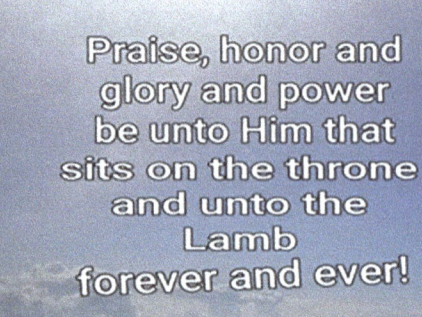

Chapter 59

THE GREAT FEAST

Jesus shared this parable:

There was a man who invited many to join him in a great feast. When the day for the feast arrived, the host instructed his servant to notify all the invited guests and tell them, "Come, for everything is now ready for you!" But one by one they all made excuses. One said, "I can't come. I just bought some property and I'm obligated to go and look it over." Another said, "Please accept my regrets, for I just purchased five teams of oxen and I need to make sure they can pull the plow."

Another one said, "I can't come because I just got married."

The servant reported back to the host and told him of all their excuses. So the master became angry and said to his servant, "Go at once throughout the city and invite anyone you find—the poor, the blind, the disabled, the hurting, and the lonely—and invite them to my banquet."

When the servant returned to his master, he said, "Sir, I have done what you've asked, but there's still room for more."

So the master told him, "All right. Go out again, and this time bring them all back with you. Persuade the beggars on the streets, the outcasts, even the homeless. Urgently insist that they come in and enjoy the feast so that my house will be full." I say to you all, "THE ONE WHO RECEIVES AN INVITATION TO FEAST WITH ME AND MAKES

THE GREAT FEAST

EXCUSES WILL NEVER ENJOY MY BANQUET."
Luke 14:16-24, TPT
(Emphasis Mine)

Now I invite you to a FEAST prepared by Jesus. Have you received Him as your Lord and Savior? He is coming soon, and He will take us to a great banquet. PLEASE ACCEPT HIS INVITATION! DON'T BE TOO BUSY AND MAKE EXCUSES!

If you would like to receive Jesus, repeat this prayer:

Jesus, I am a sinner, and I ask You to forgive my sins. I receive You now. Come into my heart and write my name in the Book of Life. Amen!

If you said this prayer from your heart, you are now a child of God. Get a Bible and start reading the New Testament every day. Find a good church that moves in the

Holy Spirit, and go as often as the doors are open.

If you need healing in your body today, receive it right now in the name of Jesus!

AUTHOR CONTACT PAGE

You may contact Linda Delgado directly in the following way:

allnations33@yahoo.com

www.ingramcontent.com/pod-product-compliance
Lightning Source LLC
Chambersburg PA
CBHW040305170426
43194CB00022B/2908